MOTHERS MATTER

AN ANALYSIS OF OBJECT RELATIONS, MOTHER-CHILD DYADS

BY
DR. ROBERT E. GORRELL

Llumina Press

ISBN: 1-59526-244-X
Printed in the United States of America by Llumina Press

To the following mothers and the invaluable lessons each taught me:

Nora: God is a partner in every dream.
Emily: God answers prayers.
Prudy: Joy is an act of Christian witness.
Tiffany: Hope is an act of faith.
Stacye: Courage is the foundation of faith, not perfection.

ACKNOWLEDGEMENTS

I would like to thank Dr. Rick Walston, my mentor and teacher at Columbia Evangelical Seminary. Dr. Curtis Nigh and Dr. Michael D. Potts have been invaluable in their contributions to my understanding of Christian counseling. I also wish to express my appreciation to Dr. Robert Outlaw and Mrs. Bettie Black for their guidance and assistance in helping me develop counseling ministries within the local church. I am also grateful to Dr. George Warren for helping me understand the role of the pastor as teacher.

This work sought to bring a greater understanding to the role of parents in raising children. In D. W. Winnicott, I found something of my mother's optimism and sense of adventure. As did my mother, Winnicott believed in helping others, especially children. He provided me with an understanding of how my mother got the job of parenting done. Through Winnicott, I came to understand that my mother was an amazing person long before I realized it. I use the theory developed by this researcher almost daily as a pastor, as well as just another individual making my way through this world. Winnicott reminds me that, in every adult, there is a child we must acknowledge.

Flannery O'Connor provides a context for life as I understand it. O'Connor describes the world of my father's family. As she depicts failing people, her illustrations also often portray how these individuals prevail despite their personal flaws. For O'Connor, courage is the ultimate virtue, and such virtue is based upon a deep faith in God.

PREFACE

This study focuses on two short stories by Flannery O'Connor to explore the theory of D. W. Winnicott related to early childhood development. This study found that the inherited potential of individuals is determined by the quality of their early maternal environment, especially during the first two paradoxical stages of development defined by Winnicott—'absolute dependence' and 'relative dependence'. The mother/adult-child relationships depicted by O'Connor in her two short stories of focus in this research—"Good Country People" and "The Enduring Chill"—serve as case studies in this investigation. The study examines the ramifications of 'not good-enough' mothering on the psychological state of the infant during these first two stages of development. The concepts of mirroring, impingement, true- and false-self development, illusion, transitional phenomenon, and aggression are all considered within the context of the mother-child dyad to demonstrate how maternal inadequacy undermines all aspects of what Winnicott termed the 'going-on-being' of the child.

It is determined that the protagonist in "The Enduring Chill," Asbury Fox, was psychologically fixated at the stage of absolute dependence because he exhibited symptoms indicative of repetitive, early-environmental impingement. He was maternally dependent with little or no sense of self, exhibited primitive omnipotence, and thwarted creativity. Conversely, Joy/Hulga Hopewell in "Good Country People" achieved the developmental stage of relative dependence, based upon her ability to physically and psychologically separate from her mother, forge her own identity, accomplish educational goals, and make use of transitional objects.

In conjunction with the observation of mother-infant dyads, the impact of the absent father is also assessed in determining the level of impairment and quality in the ultimate achievement of independence by the adult child. This study demonstrates that Asbury Fox was unable to complete passage of the Oedipus complex because his father died when he was five. The divorce of her parents when Joy/Hulga was ten years of age, left her without a father to mediate in her relationship with her mother. Thus, these two angry adult children experienced either dependency, as exhibited by Asbury Fox who searches for fathers throughout his life, or rejection of maternal closeness, as exhibited by Joy/Hulga who attempted to forge a father in the creation of a new name.

CONTENTS

CHAPTER 1

INTRODUCTION

This investigation explores the environmental impact of early infancy on the subsequent emotional and creative potential of adults. The study examines the importance of motherhood as both the environment and object within the mother-infant relationship. The dynamics within this pivotal relationship that inhibit the growth of the infant during the first two phases of development—the "absolute dependence" of the newborn (Winnicott 1960a, 43) and the "relative dependence" of the toddler (46)—is also investigated. 'Paradox' is a crucial concept during these two developmental stages as conflicting beliefs merge in opposition to create ultimate growth potential. Ogden (1986) explained, "Many of Winnicott's most valuable clinical and theoretical contributions are in the form of paradoxes that he asks us to accept without resolving, for the truth of the paradox lies in neither of its poles, but in the space between them" (168). Winnicott (1967b) further emphasized the importance of paradox as he described the omnipotent creation of the object from the perspective of the infant in the following excerpt: "A paradox is involved here, in that in this initial phase the baby creates the object, but the object is already there, else he would not have created it. The paradox has to be accepted, not resolved" (30). Paradoxes are examined within the context of initial ego union with, and gradual separation from, the mother including (a) both the oneness and separateness of the mother and infant during "primary material preoccupation" (Winnicott 1960a, 28) in absolute dependence, and (b) the move toward independence made by the infant during the period of relative dependence. The latter stage involves the use of transitional space and transitional phenomena leading to the capacity of the infant to be alone in the presence of the mother, as well as the ultimate ability to distinguish between internal and external reality. This study also examines the importance of the father during these two initial phases of life. In particular, it discusses how the absence of the father affects the mother-infant dyad, principally the ability of the infant to separate from the mother.

The writings and research of D. W. Winnicott were selected as a focus in this study because of the optimistic belief this investigator portrays in the resilience of the average individual. Rather than concentrating on rigid paradigms that 'force-fit' individuals to theory, Winnicott tailors theory to individuals. He stated, "It is not enough for [an] analyst to state that the external factor is recognized as having its importance. If a formulation of a complete child psychology is being made, one that can be tested by direct observation, the analyst must imaginatively clothe the earliest material presented by the patient with the environment, the environment that is implied but which the patient cannot give in analysis because of never having been aware of it" (Winnicott 1957, 113). Winnicott (1967b) later stated, "I'm going to show that infants are ill very early, and if the theory doesn't fit it, it's just got to adjust itself" (575).

As a pediatrician, Winnicott (1957) observed the emotional effects of mothering styles upon infants firsthand. He strove to assist mothers in creating positive environments for their infants by guiding them in his private practice and through publishing articles and serving as a keynote speaker on radio programs and public seminars. Rather than isolating himself within the scholarly towers of academia, Winnicott became an external proponent of education by his proactive delivery of information to the average individual. He also trained psychiatric analysts to serve as surrogate mothers just 'good enough' for effective analysis in the cultivation of the potential growth thwarted by a poor environmental beginning. Winnicott (1960a) explained, "My thesis is that what we do in therapy is to attempt to imitate the natural process that characterizes the behavior of any mother of her own infant. If I am right, it is the mother-infant couple that teach us the basic principles on which we may base our therapeutic work, when we are treating children whose early mothering was 'not good enough', or was interrupted" (19–20). Adult children from such adverse early beginnings are often seen in analysis, tenaciously hiding behind the façade of an adult. The approach described by Winnicott has much to offer therapists/analysts seeking to assist patients uncover their creative potential.

The majority of ideas presented by Winnicott (1960a) are delivered in an informal style to both lay people and colleagues. His writing is simple, yet eloquently builds upon concepts that are transformations of earlier psychoanalytic thought—in particular, that of Freud and Klein (as cited in Greenberg and Mitchell 1983). Rather than consider the infant as a unique and separate being with biological drives and motivations, Winnicott was one of the first theorists to understand the mother and infant as a single unit within which neither exists without the other. Winnicott was also one of the first theorists to not only make analysis available to the middle class, but most importantly, to pioneer the significance of the mother-infant relationship to the subsequent development of all individuals.

Classical analytic theory delved into the childhood experiences of adults—what Davis and Wallbridge (1981) refer to as "experience seen backwards" (71). In contrast, Winnicott (1939b) began observational studies of children within the clinical setting, which was a new practice. Whereas Freudian theory focused on the psychoneuroses of adults related to their childhood interactions with both parents, Winnicott studied the influence of the early or pre-Oedipal mother as both environment and object on the infant, and later, on the adult. As Winnicott pointed out, "At that time, in the 1920s, everything had the Oedipus complex at its core. The analysis of the psychoneuroses led the analyst over and over again to the anxieties belonging to the instinctual life at the four to five year period in the child's relationship to the two parents. . . . Now innumerable case histories showed me that the children who became disturbed, whether psychoneurotic, psychotic, or antisocial, showed difficulties in their emotional development in infancy. . . . Something was wrong somewhere" (as cited in Davis and Wallbridge 1981, 17).

Literature as a Teaching Tool

Literature is an especially fitting medium to study the research of Winnicott (1957) who encouraged the development of creativity. Other issues prompted the selection of literature over actual case studies. First, for purposes of this particular study, literature provided the liberty to select the most distorted examples of mother-infant disruptions as teaching tools to discuss the Winnicott (1957) theory. Second, literature imposes no boundary violation of an actual therapist-patient relationship on such research (Glover 1998). Rather, it allows for a neutral stance, much like the function of the implicit father in the mother-infant relationship, as it mediates through fiction a very real problem. Consequently, any potential conflict with regard to confidentiality between the patient and therapist is removed.

Similar to Winnicott (1964a, 1964b, 1965), O'Connor (1979a, 1979b) used the medium of paradox as an undefined tension ultimately leading to some form of change. The following quote from Jung found amongst the belongings of O'Connor after her death, portrays the importance, beauty, and elusiveness of paradox: "A great work of art is like a dream, for all its apparent obviousness it does not explain itself and is never unequivocal" (as cited in Kinney 1985, 89). Greenberg and Mitchell (1983) best described the paradoxical nature of development in the Winnicott theory as a "continuously hazardous struggle of the self for an individuated existence, which at the same time allows for intimate contact with others" (190). Winnicott (1967b) emphasized the importance of paradox as he described the omnipotent creation of the object by infants. He stated, "A paradox is involved here, in that in this initial phase the baby creates the object, but the object is already there, else he would not have created it. The paradox has to be accepted, not resolved" (30).

The intensity and intelligence of American writer Flannery O'Connor (1979a, 1979b), can often overwhelm readers. As a Southern female writer, on a par with the best-selling American author, William Faulkner, she exposed the foibles of human behavior. It seemed logical, therefore, that the protagonists in her short stories would serve as excellent case studies for this current research, especially because she created the most exquisitely disturbed, almost grotesque, mother-child dyads. McFarland (1976) described the term 'grotesque' as "physically or psychically abnormal, and bizarre and extreme situations, especially those in which contradictory elements, such as comedy and horror, are mixed" (3). "The Enduring Chill"—an O'Connor (1979a) short story—provided an example of mother-infant relationship failure as the protagonist is firmly embedded within the developmental phase of absolute dependence. The protagonist in "Good Country People" fashions a kind of crude separation leading to relative dependence (O'Connor 1979b). O'Connor (n.d.) wrote, "I myself prefer to say that a story is a dramatic event that involves a person because he is a person, and a particular person – that is because he shares in the general human condition and in some specific human situation. A story always involves [in] a dramatic way, the mystery of the personality" (90).

The two named stories are the literature of focus for this current research and reflect a surface reality while simultaneously revealing the distortions of the characters through allegory and exaggeration (O'Connor 1979a, 1979b). For example, to make a point, an author may overstate a situation to comical proportions. O'Connor practices this in a formidable manner within the two stories cited as she pits her mother characters and their children against each other in an almost primal struggle for survival. According to O'Connor (1960), the novelist must "know how far he can distort without destroying, and in order not to destroy, he will have to descend far enough into himself to reach those underground springs that give life to his work" (50). As Winnicott (1967c) described, "Much of the pleasure in experience of art in one form or another arises from the nearness to unintegration to which the artist's creation may safely lead the audience or viewer. So where the artist's achievement is potentially great, failure near the point of achievement may cause great pain to the audience by bringing them close to disintegration or the memory of disintegration, and leaving them there. The appreciation of art thus keeps people on a knife-edge, because achievement is so close to painful failure. This experience must be reckoned part of health" (29).

Synthesis of Psychoanalytic Theory and Literature

Literature serves as a 'mirror' of life through the analysis of character development. Using the Winnicott (1957) theory as an interpretive lens for the O'Connor (1979a, 1979b) stories provides a creative space for understanding the theory. Moreover, examination of the Winnicottian elements woven deeply within these American, although fictionalized, families with their mother-child dyads illuminates aspects of the therapeutic tasks and challenges facing contemporary American clinicians. By focusing on the two developmental stages of absolute dependence and relative dependence while reading these stories as case histories, a mental vision emerges of how symptoms manifest in the psychological development of individuals.

The powerful reactions evoked by "The Enduring Chill" (O'Connor 1979a) and "Good Country People" (O'Connor 1979b) pull at the most primitive of emotional states, reflecting the capacity and need for inter-action. As mentioned earlier, the protagonists in these stories are firmly embedded in a primitive psychological state somewhere between what Winnicott (1960b) referred to as primary "unintegration," (18) or the synonymous "true self," and "integration" (148). An analogy of uninte-gration might be the depiction of a child playing in the presence of the mother and, at the same time, quite isolated and contained in self (i.e., integration)—an 'I am' status typically attained by the end of the first year of life (Winnicott 1958). Disruption of the evolutionary process from unintegration to integration is indicative of unhealthy environ-mental beginnings.

The psychodynamic analysis of the O'Connor (1979a, 1979b) ficti-tious stories explores the impact of 'not good-enough' mothering as illustrated through the unique bonding and relational breakdowns be-tween two adult children and their mothers, in conjunction with the absence of the fathers. The protagonists from the stories serve as case studies for the Winnicott (1972) relational model, which can effectively facilitate an understanding of how and why these characters, and many real people, struggle to interact in the world with deficient personali-ties. 'Deficient' does not necessarily equate to a biological predisposition to failure reflected in unsatisfactory interaction with the environment. Rather, from the Winnicott perspective, failure in early environmental nurturing on the part of the mother or primary caretaker forms 'cracks' in the foundational object relations of the infant, which are then 'played out' in the psychological life and interpersonal rela-tionships of the child as an adult.

The two O'Connor (1979a, 1979b) stories used to illuminate the Winnicott (1972) theory demonstrate the described psychodynamic. Both protagonists struggle to interact with hostile environments, and both are developmentally immature. One of the protagonists, Joy/Hulga Hopewell, is able to create a crude transitional space despite poor envi-ronmental beginnings. The other protagonist, Asbury Fox, is frozen in time, unable to achieve the "intermediate area . . . between primary creativity and objective perception based on reality-testing" (Winnicott 1961, 239) and, therefore, that region between illusion and reality. The creative insights of both Winnicott and O'Connor into the human ex-perience are based upon their observations, experiences, and beliefs;

each leaves a legacy of unique visions in their writings. O'Connor (1960) stated, "The Southern writer is forced from all sides to make his gaze extend beyond the surface, beyond mere problems, until it touches that realm which is the concern of prophets and poets" (45). Winnicott (1961) also espoused that communication and understanding must "be transmitted and that the limitations and blind spots [of the troubled individual] will very definitely affect the way he is able to show what he sees" (46).

The two stories cited in this investigation serve as case studies for the examination of character development (O'Connor 1979a, 1979b). Although the stories are fictional, the experiences and underpinning theory depict reality for many individuals. Applying the Winnicott (1961) theoretical model to this investigation provided a foundation upon which to understand the importance of early development on behavior later in life. For example, O'Connor (1979a) uses the bird stain in "The Enduring Chill" as both an unfriendly and indifferent symbol of the character of the mother. One could easily envision a large, terrifying bird with talons outstretched and, at the same time, realize that a stain on the ceiling is just that—a stain on the ceiling. The tension between the emotional and visual content revealed through the protagonist in this story is how O'Connor communicates with the reader. In the theory of Winnicott, the infant is both contained and frustrated, but the loss of equilibrium occurring from the failure is so minimal that it is barely discernible. That insignificant loss is the psychological balance necessary to allow psychic growth and creativity to emerge, just as the tension in the story needs to exist to keep the reader engaged. Winnicott(1971b) explained,

> My contribution is to ask for a paradox to be accepted and tolerated and respected and not to be resolved. By flight to split off intellectual functioning, it is possible to resolve the paradox, but the price of this is the loss of the value of the paradox itself.
>
> This paradox, once accepted and tolerated, has value for every human individual who is not only alive and living in this world but who is also capable of being infinitely enriched by exploitation of the cultural link with the past and with the future. (xii)

Literature as Focus

D. W. Winnicott

Donald Woods Winnicott was born in 1896 in England to an upper-middle-class family. His father, a successful merchant specializing in women's corsetry (Phillips 1988, 23), was forty-two when Winnicott was born. Despite his financial and social achievements, his father, who was knighted Mayor of Plymouth, was self-conscious about his lack of education; in part, due to learning difficulties. He therefore engaged in local politics rather than parliament. He was extremely preoccupied and spent a great deal of time away from home, becoming a "rather bland figure" (20) in the life of his son. In a letter to his wife, Winnicott revealed, "So my father was there to kill and be killed, but it is probably true that in my early years he left me too much to all my mothers. Things never quite righted themselves" (as cited in Winnicott 1978, 3). Consequently, according to Phillips, "Fathers turn up in his writings as brackets or parentheses" (6).

Winnicott described his mother as "vivacious and outgoing and was able to show and express her feelings easily" (as cited in Winnicott, 1978, 1). Winnicott was the youngest child and only boy, with two sisters who were several years older. The age discrepancy was said to be enough to cause him to feel as though he were an only child. This position may be responsible for descriptions of Winnicott years later as "a loner and sometimes difficult" (Grolnick 1990, 12). The catalyst to his decision toward a career in medicine at the beginning of World War I was a sports-related injury at age fifteen while away at boarding school. He was sent away to school because his father believed Winnicott was falling in with the wrong crowd when his father overheard him use the term "drat" (Hughes 1990, 18).

Life was full of paradox for Winnicott, according to Prince Masud Khan who stated, "He grew up much loved and pampered by his parents and two elder sisters. If he was loved much, much was also expected of him. So paradox, as he was to call it himself, started from the beginning of his life, in his living, in very many ways" (as cited in Clancier and Kalmanovitch 1984, xvi). Early on, Winnicott was enamored with the work of Darwin. His developmental theory seems modeled on this evolutionary system as the healthy infant negotiateed a series of complex stages of development, gradually adapting to the surrounding environment. Paradoxically, in order for the infant to achieve 'going-on-being'—the process of ego development leading toward a sense of self as separate—the environment must initially adapt completely to the infant.

Winnicott's first wife, according to Khan, was "a beautiful operatic singer, went mad, and taking care of her took all his youth. But during that time he did establish himself as a clinician in psychotherapy with children" (as cited in Clancier and Kalmanovitch 1984, xvi). His second marriage to Clare Winnicott was a playful and collaborative one lasting until he died in 1971 (Goldman 1993). Kahn stated, "The paradox that haunted D.W.W . . . was that living and dying were of the same fabric made" (as cited in Clancier and Kalmanovitch 1984, xvi). Although Winnicott spent his life caring for and studying children, he had none of his own.

During World War I, Winnicott served in the Navy as a surgeon probationer (Hughes 1990, 19). Following the war, he returned to England to resume studying medicine. He began his medical career in 1921 as a pediatric consultant at two different hospitals for children, experiencing an increasing fascination with infant-mother interactions, while always maintaining his major interest in psychoanalysis. He ultimately incorporated both fields in the psychoanalytic treatment of children and adults (Clancier and Kalmanovitch 1984; Goldman 1993; Grolnick 1990). The interest demonstrated by Winnicott in the influence of the environment on the psychological growth of infants was intensified by the Second World War. It was during this time that he learned firsthand how delinquency was linked to deprivation, observing children whose antisocial behavior prevented them from placement in foster homes (Grolnick 1990, 14). He realized how "interpretation must be accompanied by careful attention to the environment and how important holding and handling and a good enough setting were for normal development to take place, or for there to be a chance for the correction of abnormal development" (15). Winnicott incorporated these observations in his own psychoanalytic theory and practice. His theory was "rooted in 'direct' observation of infants and children and those who cared for them; and 'indirect' observation made during the course of psychoanalysis of patients of all ages" (Davis and Wallbridge 1981, 19).

Winnicott first encountered psychoanalytic writings as he researched ways to help him recall dreams as a medical student in 1971 (Weisberg 1994). He began a ten-year analysis with James Strachey in 1923 to overcome shyness (Hughes 1989). During the following decade, the British Psycho-Analytic Society endured many changes. In 1925, Melanie Klein was invited to lecture at the Society by Ernest Jones, at the insistence of Alex and James Strachey. By 1926, Klein was firmly implanted in London's psychoanalytic society. Winnicott was encouraged by Strachey to cultivate an alliance with Klein because she was a respected analyst, also specializing in children. Consequently, in the 1930s, Winnicott—the only pediatrician applying psychoanalytic theory to children—became a student of Klein in an extensive supervisory relationship while analyzing the son of Klein. Winnicott and Klein enjoyed a very close relationship until the beginning of World War II. During that time, he also began a six-year analysis with Joan Riviere, Klein's closest collaborator (Greenberg and Mitchell 1983); although according to Winnicott's widow, he really desired his second analysis to be with Klein (Hughes 1990).

By 1938, the composition and nature of the British Psycho-Analytic Society had changed enormously with a pre-World War II influx of émigré analysts fleeing Central Europe for London. These foreign analysts comprised one third of the Society by 1938. The inflow of new members with opposing theoretical views caused dissent within the organization, ultimately splitting the group into two separate factions— those loyal to Anna Freud and those following Melanie Klein. Winnicott joined a third fraction—the Independent British School—also known as simply the Middle School. This group included such luminaries as Fairbairn, Marion Milner, and John Bowlby, and refused to pledge allegiance to either Klein or Freud (Weisberg 1994). Rather, they adopted a 'middle-ground' position, preferring to side with neither the Freudian nor Kleinian camp.

Winnicott paid a great price for his independence as a participant in the Middle School group. Although he served as president of the Society for two terms—from 1956 to 1959 and from 1965 to 1969—he was excluded from the Kleinian circle, even though he revered Klein. Despite this exclusion, Winnicott continued to evolve his own theory of development based upon interactions between infants and their environments. This theory continued to grow out of his interest in 'manifest psychosis' (Hughes 1990, 20). His neutral position within the Society, combined with his theory of infant ego-related, environmental dependence rendered him an outcast with the Kleinians. Because he did not adhere to the view of Klein that the infant is born with an internal object world, he was considered unqualified and barred from teaching

Kleinian theory. Despite Klein's treatment of Winnicott, he longed for her acceptance. Hughes described the relationship in the following manner: "They [had] been described as performing a pas de duex in the later 1940s and 1950s: 'Klein was the ballerina to whom Winnicott was constantly offering something, which she rejected with a toss of her head as if to say that she had it already. In those years he implicitly addressed his papers to her'" (20).

While exciting and revolutionary, the concepts of Winnicott are often characterized as disjointed, forming no organized theoretical model. Summers (1994) stated, "Although Winnicott did not present his thought in a clearly organized manner, being vague and even inconsistent at times, he espoused a consistent concept of development throughout his work, and his views on psychopathology and treatment emanate from this development scheme" (137). A facet of the disjointed quality associated with the Winnicott theory may derive from the fact that he was not allowed a formal stage, such as a classroom, upon which to present his ideas. However, the very nature of his topic also reflects this disjointed characteristic—paradoxes that cannot be resolved. Despite the fact that his innovative concepts for the treatment and understanding of psychopathology were shunned by Kleinians, his work prevailed. His developmental constructs were noted in articles, letters, and speeches assembled and printed in book form. Today, the Winnicott relational theory is considered both sound and consistent.

Flannery O'Connor

Mary Flannery O'Connor (1957) was born in 1925 in Savannah, Georgia during the Depression and in the midst of increasing Southern regionalism and isolation. She was the only child of Edward Francis and Regina Cline O'Connor. Her creativity was evident as a child in her imaginative writing and other artistic renderings. Reared a Catholic in a predominantly Protestant community, she attended parochial schools and subsequently a college for women. After receiving her master's degree in fine arts with a major in creative writing from an Iowa university, she was invited to attend a writer's colony in New York.

With the exception of the duration of time away at school, and for three years following school while living in New York and Connecticut between 1947 and 1950, O'Connor (1957) spent her life in Georgia. She resided primarily in rural Georgia on the family dairy farm inherited by her mother. Her father lived away from home from 1938 through 1940, working in Atlanta as a real-estate appraiser for the Federal Housing Administration. During those two years, her mother ran the farm on her own. The theme of the absent father is predominant in both "The Enduring Chill" (O'Connor 1979a) and "Good Country People" (O'Connor 1979b). Upon retiring in 1940, O'Connor's (1957) father moved back home; however, he died from complications of lupus a year later at age forty-one. O'Connor was fifteen years of age at the time of his death. From an early age, she was curious about the peculiar. At five, she had a chicken that gained national notoriety because it could walk both backwards and forwards (Fickett and Gilbert 1986). O'Connor (1961) ultimately chose to raise peacocks because of their beauty and mythological tie to Hera, wife of Zeus, and she was particularly fascinated by peafowl that possessed bizarre characteristics such as peacocks with one green and one orange eye. A loner, she spent hours playing with these birds, dressing them up in clothing so they resembled freakish children. Many of her literary characters possess characteristics similar to these arrogant fowl.

As an adult author, O'Connor adhered to the writing standards of the New Critics—a highly structured style of writing that she perceived as focused on "seeing that your thoughts and feelings—whatever they were—were aptly contained within your elected image" (as cited in Eigen 1985, 7). The technique appeared simplistic on the surface; however, it was actually quite complex with organized, dynamic tension between "the literal sense of the work and its implications—between that which is denoted and that which is connoted; between the concrete level and the abstract" (7). Paulson (as cited in Eigen 1985) stated that "the New Critics felt defensive in a technological age that seemed to reduce art to the didactum of its moral message or to useless decoration. . . . [Hence, the New Critic usually abandoned] the writer's biography, the readers emotional response to the work, the work's historical setting or its significance as it relates to such disciplines as psychology, philosophy, or sociology – although many critics do consider such contexts after first focusing on the structure of the work itself. The only valid means of understanding the work is to study its formal aspects, according to these critics" (8). The focus of New Critic writers was on paradox, understatement, irony, ambiguity, form, style, and implied meaning. The New Critic expected readers to tackle the complexities of this literary form and to attempt to comprehend the numerous skillful factors involved in its creation. The writings of O'Connor reflect the efficiency of this style, utilizing a complex tension between concreteness and abstraction as it distorts human behavior, highlighting the grotesque aspects in us all.

It seems apparent that O'Connor (1979a, 1979b) projected her own life into the two short stories of focus in this current research. In "Good Country People," lupus is transformed into heart disease. The main character and O'Connor are both crippled, and both are under long-term death sentences after returning home from success in the wider world. O'Connor was struck with lupus at twenty-five years of age. For eleven years, she intermittently suffered from complications of the disease until she was forced to return home to the care of her mother. At that time, the debilitating symptoms of the same disease that had killed her father ten years earlier became incapacitating and doctors gave her three years to live. In a letter to William Sessions, O'Connor (1956) drew a comparison between herself and her character, Hulga.

Similar to art and the theory developed by Winnicott (1957), writing represents a connection between internal and external states. O'Connor (1957) explained, "Art requires a delicate adjustment of the outer and inner worlds in such a way that, without changing their nature, they can be seen through each other. To know oneself is to know one's region. It is also to know the world, and it is also, paradoxically, a form of exile from the world" (33). During the time O'Connor was confined after returning home with lupus, she completed nine stories. She died in 1964 at the age of thirty-nine, leaving behind a legacy of two novels and thirty-one short stories, in addition to critiques, speeches, letters, and a growing reputation as one of the finest Southern writers. The recurring themes of sickness, impending death, absent fathers, returning home, delineation between internal and external states, and struggles with separation from mothers (i.e., Winnicottian themes) are played out in the two short stories examined in this study (O'Connor 1979a, 1979b). An analysis of O'Connor in relation to her characters is a topic of interest for possible future investigation; however, this aspect is beyond the scope of this current research. Nor are the religious beliefs of O'Connor explored, particularly the elements of grace and mystery, which are richly woven into her stories and probably sourced in her devotion to Catholicism. This study remains focused on the Winnicott theory of ego development.

Organization of the Study

This research defines the parameters of the two developmental stages of absolute dependence and relative dependence and provides a brief description of the third stage, relative independence (Winnicott 1948). It focuses on the psychological needs of infants who are totally dependent upon the environment for survival. During this early stage of life, ego is merged with that of the mother. The concepts explored are the holding environments, fusion, the good-enough mother, the importance of the father, mirroring, aggression, and paradox. In Stage Two of relative dependence, infants are moving toward separation from the fused ego state with the mother toward independence. Areas discussed in this regard are the transitional object, transitional space, and the false self. Failures of the environment during these two phases are also examined.

The O'Connor (1979a) short story, "The Enduring Chill," is explored as a case study to examine failures in mother-child interactions that are associated with the phase of absolute dependence. The short story, "Good Country People" (O'Connor 1979b), is also examined to report on the Winnicott second stage of relative dependence. Observation of the interactions within the mother/adult-child dyads of these stories provide invaluable insight into this developmental stage. The importance of the fathers in negotiation of these two stages is also addressed. In conclusion, an overview of the importance of the environment experienced by either infants or adults within the analytic setting is discussed along with the dichotomy of art and science and the importance of art in the science of art.

CHAPTER 2

METHODS

L oss of "inherited potential" (Winnicott 1960b, 43) is a tragic injury. Winnicott examined the interaction of mother-infant dyads to explain the nature of this type of injury, which occurs during the dependent stages of infant development. 'Dependence' is defined by Winnicott "as the inherited potential of an infant [who] cannot become an infant unless linked to maternal care" (43). In this situation, the infant is defined as "a very young child [including] the child up to the age of passing the Oedipus complex" (43). The Oedipus complex, according to Winnicott (1958), is the "first maturity between 2-5, when a child becomes a whole person" (103). At this point, the child becomes part of a three-person relationship in the classical sense, which is "a relationship between three persons, each felt to be a whole person by the child" (101). Winnicott (1961) believed that children who were "well cared for and who were healthy [developed] what is called the Oedipus complex . . . the capacity to be able to deal with triangular relationships—to accept the full force of the capacity to love and the complications that result" (146). A child who is unable to complete the Oedipus complex remains in a "two-body relationship with the mother" (Winnicott 1958, 29), indicating maturation of an earlier stage of development.

Although his early focus was on children, the theoretical investigations conducted by Winnicott (1946) also enlarged the scope of understanding surrounding adult behavior. He observed that the mother, who is psychically willing to release her infant from the merged state of absolute dependence, impedes the psychic growth of her infant, hinders creativity, and limits the interpersonal development. The child in this state has "not yet separated out from the subject. This is a condition to which the word merging is applied"

(Winnicott 1971a, 130). Giovacchim (1984) elaborated on this idea, referring to this merged state as "symbiotic fusion"—the traumatic experience of the infant whose mother uses him "as a narcissistic extension of herself" (84). This type of maternal impingement dominates the psyche of the infant, preventing ego integration and fostering dependence.

In his clinical practice, Winnicott (1939b) observed the repercussions of maternal domination in children and adults who 'hid' their true selves behind intellectualism, antisocial behavior, depression, and psychotic behavior. He witnessed a sense of failure and despair in adult patients who experienced poor environmental beginnings as infants. One possible failure for these adults, as children, was the inability to negotiate a series of developmental tasks leading to a sense of self, described by Winnicott as "going-on-being" (21). Giovacchim (1984) synthesized and located the symptoms of merging described by Winnicott, noting the three following common features: (a) "poorly structuralized self-representation [with] blurred boundaries" between internal and external realities; (b) "tenuous identity" (i.e., not knowing ones place within the "general scheme of things"); and (c) "little sense of self as distinct and separate" (Winnicott 1961, 84).

Manifest psychosis is beyond the scope of this study, which refers to illnesses associated with the earliest phase of development that Giovacchim (1984) referred to as "presymbiotic," where the needs of such infants were not met at all (9). Rather, this study focuses on the first two stages of development described by Winnicott (1963b) where the earliest physical needs were met, but where the environmental mother was unable to "build up . . . the personality in earliest childhood and infancy" (220). Accordingly, the infant is "never related to as a person with a mind of its own with distinct needs, [and as such, there is a] lack of cohesiveness of self-representation" due to defective mothering; the needs of the infant ego have not been met (Giovacchim 1984, 84). The mother in this situation treats the child as a "self-object" (Boyer and Giovacchim 1967, 269).

Giovacchim (1984) added to the Winnicott theory when he observed, "Children who experience such a symbiotic phase usually develop a hateful image of themselves. They revile themselves because of their badness and are, in general, self-destructive" (84). Psychiatric patients within this phase may exhibit the polarities between psychotic and sane behavior that Giovacchim refers to as "phenomenological antitheses" (82). Winnicott (1963b) explained,

Psychosis may be looked at as illness that has more to do with the experiences in the earlier phases than the tensions at the level of interpersonal relationships which lead to repressive defenses. In the extreme case there has been no true Oedipus complex because the individual was so much caught up in an earlier stage of development that true and full-blooded triangular relationships never became a fact.

Of course you will find cases to describe in which there is a mixture of normality in terms of the Oedipus complex and of psychosis in terms of being stuck at a phase of early emotional development. (219)

Winnicott (1965) espoused that the initial sense of "I" develops out of the "facilitating matrix" (19) of the mother-infant unit. This crucial interaction 'sets the stage' for optimal ego growth and potential development of self for the infant. This merged mother-infant concept is unlike those views espoused by Freud and Klein (as cited in Davis and Wallbridge 1981). Winnicott believed that the infant, as a separate psychological entity, does not really exist at birth. Freud, on the other hand, believed that, in the infant, is born innate psychic capabilities, while Klein theorized that the "phantasies and anxieties concerning the state of one's internal object world are the underlying basis for one's behavior, moods and sense of self" (as cited in Greenberg and Mitchell 1983, 121). Both Freud and Klein believed that the infant is born with a distinctly separate identity and sense of self.

Winnicott (1960b) posited that healthy psychological differentiation occurs during what he referred to as the holding phase of development, and through the negotiation of a series of three stages of mother-infant interactions in which intimacy, separation, and differentiation are learned. 'Healthy', in this sense, implies the existence of the 'id'—the 'unhealthy' unconscious and untamed part of the psyche. According to Winnicott, when "gathered into the service of the ego and the ego masters the . . . id-satisfactions become ego strengtheners" (40). The untamed id "remains relatively or totally 'external' to the ego, and id-satisfactions remain physical, and have the effect of threatening ego structure until defenses of psychotic quality are organized" (40). Winnicott also espouses that the processes that either promote or inhibit the potential development of the unique and authentic self of infants are determined by the quality of early maternal caretaking. This is what differentiates Winnicott so dramatically from Freud and Klein (as cited in Winnicott 1960a). He emphasized actual interpersonal relationships, while Freud and Klein focused on the unconscious or fantasy world of the individual.

Winnicott (1960a) referred to the first of the three stages of the holding phase of development as absolute dependence to describe a state in which "actual physical holding and also total environmental provision" take place (43). This is the phase in which the mother, through the construction and maintenance of a trustworthy physical and psychological environment, nurtures the development of the infant. Once this stage has been negotiated, the infant enters two succeeding stages—relative dependence and toward independence— within which the process of separation continues. Greenberg and Mitchell (1983) pointed out the paradoxical nature of separation as the infant matures. These researchers documented, "Through separation nothing is lost, but rather something is gained and preserved" (190). Winnicott (1963b) added, *"This is the place that I have set out to examine,* the separation that is *not* a separation but a form of union" (emphasis mine) (115).

To better understand the concept of the infant-mother matrix, it is important to first grasp the meaning of the paradox of dialectics—a tension continuously at play in the theory developed by Winnicott (1939a). His theory of opposites incorporates the concept of dialectics, a term the German philosopher Hegel used to signify a synthesis of opposing views. Hegel placed *becoming* above *being,* conceiving the world as a continually evolving process (as cited in Runes 1959). Winnicott used dialectics to epitomize opposing forces simultaneously at work in the psychological evolution of the individual. Ogden (1986) stated, "A dialectical relationship allows for a resonance of . . . conscious and unconscious meanings" (222). Winnicott (1964b) believed that the individual psyche must navigate a series of paradoxical stages of development if the real self is to be achieved—a negotiation which cannot be made without a stable "facilitating environment" (101). This environment is a safe and reliable climate that is consistently monitored and adapted to meet the unique needs of the individual infant. As the attention of the mother diminishes, infants gradually realize their independence and separate natures from their mothers. This awareness is spawned by psychological disruption that is necessary for ego development.

Winnicott (1971b) proposed that the developmental stage of absolute dependence occurs prior to objectivity and perception. He explained, "At the theoretical beginning a baby can be said to live in a subjective or conceptual world. The change from the primary state to one in which objective perception is possible is not only a matter of [an] inherent or inherited growth process; it needs in addition an environmental minimum. It belongs to the whole vast theme of the individual traveling from dependence towards independence" (151). According to Winnicott (1960a), the struggle for independence is a necessary step in infant development. Through the process of separation from the mother or caretaker, the infant matures psychologically as the self emerges. In ideal conditions, the good-enough mother, or other caretaker who adequately attends to the needs of the infant, provides a holding environment. This physical and psychic container, which protects the psychological organization of experiences for the infant, minimizes "impingements to which the infant must meet with resultant annihilation of personal being," while still allowing the infant to establish a "continuity of existence" (47). Winnicott (1948) emphasized the importance of the mother "holding the whole person in mind, so the child can then afford to be in pieces" as he progresses through primitive development (25).

The Paradoxical Process: Negotiating the Three Stages of Development within the Holding Environment

Stage One: Absolute Dependence

The stage of absolute dependence begins 'in utero' and lasts for several months following birth. Winnicott (1963b) stated that the "infant is at one and the same time dependent and independent" (84). This statement exemplifies the Winnicott theory of paradox in that both ideas contradict each other while also existing simultaneously. At this stage, the infant is both dependent and independent, yet does not experience a sense of self. In this phase of ego fusion with her infant, the healthy mother experiences similar responses of dependence and independence, but she is able to maintain her sense of self while concurrently committing herself entirely to her infant. While in utero, the infant is literally attached to the mother by the umbilical cord and is dependent upon her body for nourishment and protection. The baby and mother are physically a single unit, one contained within the other.

Toward the end of the pregnancy, the healthy mother enters into a phase Winnicott (1963b) referred to as "primary maternal preoccupation"—a state of complete devotion to the survival of her infant (73). During the initial weeks following birth, the mother serves as the emotional environment for the infant as she protects him from premature exposure to external reality and, at the appropriate time, introduces the infant to the world. The mother becomes the 'facilitating environment,' mediating between the external environment and the internal needs of the infant to avoid premature awareness of separateness. The baby and mother appear as one, even though they are physically separate beings. According to Winnicott (1960a), "There is not such thing as a baby," during this early phase (39). The mother holds the infant in her arms, her heart, and her mind, and the infant responds as though he is an extension of the mother. It might appear that the mother is caring for a part of herself as she intuitively senses the needs of the infant before those needs arise. Winnicott also stated, "The mother, through identification of herself with the infant, knows what the infant needs in the way of holding and in the provision of an environment generally" (54).

At birth, the infant is separated from its intimate physical connection with the mother, but remains reliant upon her for physical and psychological sustenance. The healthy mother also has a conscious need for physical and psychological closeness with her infant. Winnicott (1963b) asserted that, when a mother looks into the face of her infant, she sees the best qualities of herself. She both literally and figuratively places herself between her infant and the outside world, protecting not only the well-being of her child, but also preserving those positive aspects of herself. Consequently, the maturational process of the infant begins with the transition from a physical connection with the mother 'in utero', to the mother as the external environment. It could be said that, at the moment of birth, the world is turned inside out for the infant; however, as mentioned earlier, the mother prevents premature awareness of internal and external reality by surrendering to the needs of her infant as if they were one entity.

Through the adaptation of the mother to the needs of the infant, her baby experiences the breast as an extension of himself (Winnicott 1966d, 179), which he believes is under his omnipotent control. When hungry, the breast appears and the infant is nourished. This exemplifies the importance of what Winnicott described as "the mother's ability to present the world in such a way that the infant does not at first have to know that the object is not created by the infant" (179). Ogden (1986) referred to this state as the "invisible subject object," in which there is no differentiation for the infant between external and internal reality (201). The illusion is made possible by the mother who meets the needs of the infant before those needs even come to fruition, thereby protecting him from premature awareness of separateness. The paradox is the postponement of the knowledge of desire and separateness to allow presentation of reality at a subsequent and more appropriate time. Thus, the mother is simultaneously separate from and a part of the infant. She *is* the environment—a type of emotional marsupial that maintains "potential space" (Winnicott 1968b, 205) while protecting, nurturing, and fortifying the psychological integrity of her infant. 'Potential space' is defined as the area *"between a child and the mother when experience has produced in the child a high degree of confidence in the mother"* (emphasis mine) (Winnicott 1967a, 36). Not only is the infant physically defenseless following birth, but the mother is also psychologically preoccupied. In the process of adapting to the needs of her infant, the mother also becomes psychologically vulnerable and dependent (Winnicott 1963a). Consequently, both mother and infant require environmental support.

During the initial period of absolute dependence, the infant is unaware of being either separate from or connected to the environment. Neither subject nor object exists. There is no 'I.' Additionally, from the infant's perspective, there is neither 'here' nor 'there'; there just 'is'. During this phase of development, the infant ego requires a "simple matter of holding" (Winnicott 1963a, 86) when the "ego immaturity is naturally balanced by ego-support from the mother" (Winnicott 1958, 32) who is empathetically attuned to the needs and sensitivities of her infant and is both physically and emotionally responsive to them. As Winnicott (1963a) pointed out, "No one can hold a baby unless able to identify with the baby," and there is no one better equipped to do this than a mother (86). A good-enough mother makes an active adaptation to the needs of the infant and, in so doing, becomes the pivotal facilitator toward ultimate independence for the infant.

Role of the Father

Whereas infant care is received primarily from the mother, paternal sustenance also comes from the father and other family members who play important roles in freeing the mother to devote her full attention to the care of her baby. The father's role, or that of any adult who stands in primary relationship to the mother and infant, is key during this early phase of development because the mother depends upon this support individual and hold him invisibly within her mind as she cares for her infant. The infant 'takes in' the father through the mother's experience. The role of the father within the early stage of absolute dependence is through supporting and encouraging the mother. If the mother feels supported and loved by her husband, these feelings are vicariously passed along to the infant. Therefore, a silent triangular relationship exists. The father exists in the mind of the mother, and the mother subconsciously projects that fact to the infant. Davis and Wallbridge (1981) stated, "The survival of the mother enhances the capacity of the individual to take risks" (162). If a healthy build-up of "intra-psychic elements" (Winnicott 1970, 468) is gradually constructed over time, the child can then proceed through the oedipal complex. As the toddler passes through the oedipal phase—typically at approximately two to four years of age—the triangular relationship between the mother, father, and infant is at its most vivid stage and entails the capacity of the infant to view himself as a whole being among two other whole beings.

Winnicott (1968b) documented, "There is a difference according to whether the father is there or not, is able to make a relationship or not, is sane or insane, is free or rigid in personality" (242). If the father is not 'there' supporting the mother, this fact has an important impact on the mother-infant relationship. The mother is affected by the presence or absence of the father, and her moods affect the infant. Although not a detailed facet of the role of the father, Winnicott asserts that the father ultimately has a significant impact on the baby. He stated, "I suggest that the baby is likely to make use of the father as a blue-print for his or her own integration when just becoming at times a unit" (242). Another important consideration is that the mother carries infantile psychic memories of her own mother, which help sustain her through psychological merging with the infant. Consequently, in a healthy household, the entire family is responsible for the environmental condition of the infant.

Mother-infant Relationship

From the last trimester of pregnancy, through birth, and to the infancy stage of her baby, the mother remains in a state of maternal preoccupation, focused completely on the needs of her infant. Following birth, when the infant is hungry, the breast is offered. The mother creates an environment, through repeated positive experiences, within which the infant perceives the breast to be under his control. Omnipotence is the illusion. As Winnicott (1958) described it, "That the world can be created and that what is created is the world" (53). The illusion that there is no difference between internal and external reality is provided and sustained for the infant by the mother. Such illusion protects the infant from premature awareness of separateness. Therefore, if the baby has a need, such as with hunger, he will imagine the breast. At that moment, the mother offers her breast and the infant believes it was his imagination that created the object; need and object become one and the same.

Through the repeated act of the breast being created by the infant out of need, and provided by the mother out of love, the infant discovers the object (Winnicott 1958). In time, the infant learns that the object is separate from him. The mother then functions as a 'psychic mirror' for the infant by empathetically turning to the needs and sensitivities of her infant through physical and emotional responsiveness. The infant can then experience a sense of omnipotence—"I am hungry, I cry, I am fed." As time elapses and the mother intuitively, but not consciously, becomes more involved with her own needs, a diminution in the immediate gratification of the demands of the infant occurs. The result of the unwitting withdrawal by the mother results in frustration for the infant. Through frustration, discovery is generated; the object is created.

Mirroring

The mother not only functions as a psychic mirror for her infant, but also becomes a "precursor of the mirror" (Winnicott 1971b, 111). Her face is "the first mirror . . . [in] which the child can see himself or herself" (Winnicott 1967a, 497). As Winnicott (1971b) stated, "The mother is looking at the baby and what she looks like is related to what she sees there" (112). The repeated process of seeing the face of the mother react with pleasure upon each glance, grants the child new knowledge—"When I look I am seen, so I exist" (114). Winnicott (n.d.)

warns that "the child cannot use [the mother] as a mirror unless there is this principle of permissiveness to be whatever he or she is, to be himself or herself, accepted completely without evaluation or pressure to change" (497–498). Some babies see acute anxiety reflected in the faces of their mothers; for example, when mothers are depressed or dissociated from reality. Infants incorporate these feelings into their own psyches and thereby absorb a negative sense of themselves within their independence or separateness.

Ogden (1986) posited that, when the mother engages in "primary maternal preoccupation" (38) with her infant, she serves as an interpreter of the experience of her infant through the provision of what Winnicott (1967b) referred to as a "shared reality" (36). Hearing and vision assume greatly enhanced importance in Western industrialized nations where mother and baby are separated for many hours of the day. In Africa, a woman carrying her baby on her back or side is identified as an unfit mother if her baby wets or soils her after the seventh day; that is, if she cannot anticipate such elimination needs and hold the baby from her body before they occur. This finely tuned awareness of the bodily movements of the baby is almost inconceivable to those in nations where mothers and babies are separated for much of the day and sleep separately at night (Klaus and Kennell 1976, 138).

Infants interpret, through the moods of their mothers, how their mothers feel toward them, thereby learning how to feel about themselves. If, for example, the mood of the mother is depressed, the infant automatically incorporates those feelings of depression into his developing ego. A fracture occurs in the internalized reflection of the mother if the infant observes consistent sadness on the face of the mother. This splintered reflection is taken in by the infant through the eyes of the mother, or through touch or lack thereof, and incorporated into the developing sense of self. A vacant look from the mother can create a sense of abandonment for the infant.

Winnicott (1971b) stated, "If the mother face is unresponsive, then [the] mirror is a thing to be looked at but [not] to be looked into" (113). In this scenario, a reversal of roles takes place. The infant is forced into a role of primary preoccupation with the mother as a means of survival. Infants experience no sense of omnipotence in this position, for their attention is clearly focused on the needs of their mothers. They learn to monitor the faces of their mothers for cues on how to react as they adapt their behavior accordingly. These infants become both enslaved by the moods of their mothers and compliant in an effort to stay connected with the mother or primary caretaker. Delusion replaces illusion for infants within such scenarios. It is necessary for infants within the period of absolute dependence to have the illusion of omnipotence. After that, illusion becomes delusion.

According to Winnicott (1970), "The baby exists precariously in dependence on the human mother-figure. Here, and nowhere else, is an experience of omnipotence. Elsewhere omnipotence is the name given to a feeling or a delusion" (285). In earlier writings, Winnicott (1963b) presented the following detailed description:

> During the initial growth of the ego, impingement (trauma) from the environment can shatter the infant's state of being, causing him/her to prematurely experience perception of his/her separateness without the capacity to cope with this awareness. An example is the napping infant who is repeatedly jarred awake by the mother. Winnicott defines impingement as a failure at adaptation that "causes a reaction in the infant, and the reaction breaks up the going-on-being." Psychopathology evolves as a consequence of repeated impingement upon the infant's psyche during this stage. (86)

If reacting to impingements is the pattern of life for infants, serious interference ensues with the natural tendency to become an integrated unit able to cultivate self with a past, present, and future (86).

In healthy interaction between mother and infant, gradual separation is not experienced as a disastrous loss for either mother or child. Rather, the appropriate withdrawal by the mother from her infant allows them both to value separation within the context of connection, and a new relational bond is formed that is also stable and secure. This bond evolves as a result of maternal nonimpingement upon the earliest psychological development of the infant as the capacity to be alone is achieved with its own separate experiences while in the presence of the mother. In the space between mothers and infants, where illusion is created and maintained, infants gradually become aware of another presence in their lives. Illusion is the undifferentiated container where no difference exists between internal and external reality. The gradual disillusionment of the infant, through frustration, grants that infant the opportunity to creatively differentiate and accept the discrepancy between internal and external reality. For example, the infant discovers the blanket—a 'not me' thing.

According to Winnicott (1963b), human growth involves the "evolution of the ego and of the self, and includes the whole story of the id, of instincts and their vicissitudes, and of defenses in the ego relative to instinct" (39). This process encompasses the gradual sequence of separation and individuation. Winnicott refers to this growth process as going-on-being, and he further stated, "Often the child's growing up corresponds quite accurately with the mother's assumption of her own independence. A mother who cannot gradually *fail* in this matter of sensitive adaptation is failing in another sense; she is failing (because of her own immaturity or her own anxieties) to give her infant reasons for anger. An infant that has no reason for anger, but who has in him (or her) the usual amount of whatever are the ingredients of aggressiveness, is in a special difficulty, a difficulty in fusing aggression in with loving" (emphasis mine) (87).

Aggression

Winnicott (1964b) concurred with Klein that aggression is inborn. He believed it coexists with love, and has two meanings—(a) a "reaction to frustration" and (b) one of two main sources of energy (92). He believed that, from the beginning life, aggressiveness and bodily movement are equated with the ability to differentiate between what is and is not self. Infantile tactile aggression leads to a discovery of the world that is not the infant's "self, and to the beginnings of a relationship to external objects. What will quite soon be aggressive behavior is therefore at the start a simple impulse that leads to a movement and to the beginnings of exploration. Aggression is always linked in this way with the establishment of a clear distinction between what is the self and what is not the self" (94).

Winnicott (1939b) indicated that "primary aggression" is aroused by outside stimulation, such as the breast (211). In one form, the mouth of the infant acts out the aggression. Winnicott explained, the infant "bites only when he is excited and simply doesn't know what to do about it" (86). Even though the impulse is there to destroy the breast through biting or gumming the cracked nipples of the mother, there is an inhibitive response that protects the loved object by curbing these aggressive tendencies. The mother feels pain if the infant bites, and she reacts by withdrawing the breast or crying out. Her signals serve as mediating cues for acceptable and unacceptable behavior. The reaction of the mother is important as she lovingly protects herself from the aggressiveness of the infant without retaliation, while she concurrently sets limits on future behavior. In this manner, the infant has an outlet for aggressive feelings without instilling actual damage because of the limits established. The infant also learns that gratification soon follows these impulses once the aggressive impulses are satisfied.

According to Winnicott (1939b), "There is a theoretical greed or primary appetite-love, which can be cruel, hurting, dangerous, but which is so by chance. The infant's aim is gratification, peace of mind and body. Gratification brings peace, but the infant perceives that to become gratified he endangers what he loves. Normally he compromises, and allows himself enough gratification while not allowing himself to be too dangerous" (88). The infant learns that destructive impulses can lead to gratification, and that regulated impulses will not destroy the object. Winnicott further stated, "While the infant has a vast capacity for destruction it is also true that he has a vast capacity for protecting what he loves from his own destructiveness, and the main destruction must always exist in his fantasy. And the important thing to note about this instinctual aggressiveness is that . . . it is originally a part of appetite, or of some other form of instinctual love" (87).

Winnicott (1964b) later elaborated on the concept of 'magical destruction' by reporting, "This is normal to infants in the very early stages of their development, and goes side by side with magical creation. Primitive or magical destruction of all objects belongs to the fact that [for the infant] objects change from being part of 'me' to being 'not me,' from being subjective phenomena to being perceived objectively. Ordinarily such a change takes place by subtle graduation that follow the gradual changes in the developing infant, but with defective maternal provision these same changes occur suddenly, and in ways the infant cannot predict" (98).

If an infant experiences repeated frustration without gratification, anger builds and the ability to tolerate that inner reality interferes with harmonious interpersonal functioning. Accordingly, "in the early states,

when the *Me* and *Not-Me* are established, it is the aggressive compo-
nent that more surely drives the individual to a need for a *Not-Me* or an
object that is felt to be *external*" (emphasis mine) (Winnicott 1957,
215). If infants are unable to fuse aggressive and erotic impulses, they
become embedded in a destructive relationship with the mother because
aggression cannot be tolerated by her and must, therefore, be cautiously
expressed by the infant. The implied threat is that any anger directed
from the infant toward the mother will result in rejection and/or retaliation, thus potentially leading to annihilation. Anger, which is confined
to the internal structure of the body, is "unconscious except in so far as
it can be isolated by the individual from instinctual expressions"
(Winnicott 1939b, 88). Out-of-control anger is terrifying to the infant
because it represents "the dramatization of inner relation which is too
bad to be tolerated as such" (88). The infant must then learn ways of
disposing of the intolerable feelings through some type of physical or
creative outlet that is gratifying.

Winnicott (1964a) described the importance of maternal presentation of the infant to the external world in the following manner:

> By taking each infant through this vital stage in early
> development in a sensitive way, the mother gives time for
> her infant to acquire all sorts of ways of dealing with the
> shock of recognizing the existence of a world that is out-
> side his or her magical control. If time is allowed for
> maturational processes, then the infant becomes able to
> be destructive and becomes able to hate and to kick and
> to scream instead of magically annihilating that world. In
> this way actual aggression is seen to be an achievement.
> As compared with magical destruction, aggressive ideas
> and behavior take on a positive value, and hate becomes a
> sign of civilization, when we keep in mind the whole
> process of the emotional development of the individual,
> and especially the earliest stages. (98)

Summary

The major dynamic of Stage One is that there is no 'I'. No mother
and no infant; yet, there is both oneness and separateness. Ogden
(1986) referred to this developmental stage as "the period of the subjec-
tive-object" (169) in which "the mother and infant are one and the

mother and infant are two" (212). In the ideal setting, the mother is preoccupied with her infant in a fused psychic state, and as such, the mother-infant is a psychological unit composed of the primitive psychological organization of the infant and the more mature psychological organization of the mother. In unhealthy situations, infants learn too early that they are separate, and they must conform to the ramifications of that knowledge. The journey from absolute dependence to relative dependence incorporates three achievements—(a) 'integration' (i.e., ego development leading to an independent self); (b) 'personalization' (i.e., the union of psyche-soma); and (c) 'object relations' (i.e., relating to separate, whole, people) (Davis and Wallbridge 1981).

Stage Two: Relative Dependence

The healthy mother gradually introduces the external world to her infant in various ways. For example, she may not respond immediately to cries for food. Instead, she might allow herself to finish reading the last two pages of a book before responding. Such action causes infants to become more aware of their surroundings, evoking a fledgling consciousness of the self as separate from their mothers. Through such experiences, a psychic space is generated between infants and their mothers. Ogden (1986) referred to this as an "illusion that fills potential space" (201) because, paradoxically, oneness and infant separation from the mother exist concurrently.

Transitional objects and transitional space. The transitional object emerges from disillusionment (Winnicott 1966c). Through gradual withdrawal by the mother, a baby begins to develop a sense of 'me' or 'not me'—a recognition of self. As the infant becomes frustrated with the delays in gratification, the illusion of omnipotence is progressively replaced by a transitional space between mother and infant. In this space, the infant discovers a transitional object—a symbolic representative of, and substitute for, the lost mother—such as a blanket or soft toy. The object then becomes a transitional representative of maternal care—a link between internal and external reality—which is both created and discovered by the infant. This infant symbol is concrete and grounding for the children who begin to realize their limits of control and learn that an external reality exists apart from their control. This recognition becomes increasingly clear as the early preoccupation of the mother with the infant diminishes as she begins to incorporate other interests into her life. She is no longer fused in a preoccupied manner with her baby. The infant must then adapt to the shift in attention and is thus pushed toward an awareness of separateness and differentiation.

The minor frustrations arising from dosed withdrawal by the mother provide space for the infant to create and discover an object that can represent both the loss and the replacement of the mother, while also filling the gap between mother, infant, and external reality (Winnicott 1966c). Consequently, the infant must be allowed the creative illusion of the mother-infant union so the infant, as a separate being, can emerge. The mother or primary caretaker, through the initial sacrifice of self and devotion to the infant, sets the stage for the ego development of the child and the emergence of self. Consider the infant who wakes from a nap and cries for the mother. The mother does not immediately appear so the infant cries a bit longer before looking around. To his delight, he finds a soft blanket. It feels good to the touch and the baby is comforted by the feel of the blanket, just as he was when held by the mother. An important association is made. Over time, when the baby wakes up and the mother does not immediately appear, the baby grabs for the blanket and is temporarily soothed. The infant can then use the blanket to comfort himself whenever the mother is absent.

Illusion is the projection of the inner workings of an infant onto an object, and this is a crucial element in the development of the transitional object. However, the ability to create this calming illusion could not be attained without the mother gradually introducing her child to frustration. The capacity to tolerate frustration is indicative of the infant experiencing basic trust with a dependable caretaker. According to Clancier and Kalmanovitch (1984),

> The infant's ability to create the transitional object is dependent upon the gradual formation of a psychologically safe area. It is the *existence of an intermediate area, neither inside nor outside the individual, in which cultural experience will gradually become organized.* In that space, the infant exists in a state of emotional tension between knowing and not knowing of the emergence and recognition of reality. This state is a precursor to the infant's discovering his or her distinctness, and is achieved through a successful navigation of the evolution from the illusion of a merged mother-infant environment, to his/her emergence as a separate entity (emphasis mine). (90)

Individuality begins with the ability to create a transitional object. To the infant, the object represents a 'bridge' between merging with the mother and emergence of self. The success of this transition reflects a maternal ability to give the infant psyche space to grow. The transitional object replaces the mother as the 'buffer' between the developing ego of the infant and external reality, becoming both the illusion and the reality of the infant experience. The transitional object is both real and illusory. It is created within the mind of the infant and is concurrently tangible. It grows out of a safe, predictable arena created and/or encouraged by the mother or primary caretaker through patient devotion and willingness to self-sacrifice for the satisfaction and gratification of the infant. Through dosed disillusionment, the infant gradually becomes aware of his or her independence or separateness.

Winnicott (1963b) believed that the "infant in some way feels a need for the mother by knowing in his mind that mother is necessary" (86). Intense dependence upon the mother takes place for a period of six months to two years. During this time, a dialogue occurs between the infant and mother that includes language, movement, and facial mirroring. These modes of communication punctuate the growing consciousness in the infant of the meaning of separateness. Winnicott stated that "the infant exists with an inside and an outside, and a person living in the body, and more or less bounded by the skin. Once outside means 'not-ME' then inside means ME, and there is now a place in which to store things. In the child's fantasy, the personal psychic reality is located inside. If it is located outside there are good reasons" (91). Infants whose psychic realities are intruded upon by the desires of their mothers ultimately adapt to the needs of their mothers. The center of their psychic reality is located within their mothers and not within themselves. Their own psychic realities are sacrificed as they adapt to the reality of their mothers. When this occurs, the infant is making no small sacrifice. Because the infant is relinquishing his true psychic self, he is replacing it with a false two-dimensional self that lacks the potential space necessary for exploration and creative growth.

The False Self

If traumatic ruptures occur during the infant transition between oneness with the mother and the separation phase due to persistent and jarring maternal impingement, or the inability of the mother to provide immediate gratification, the infant 'shuts down' psychologically and is plunged into emotional chaos. In defense against chaos, the infant splits the budding psychological self into true and false aspects. According to Winnicott (1960b), the true self—the source of spontaneity, enthusiasm, and creativity—is unintegrated and protectively buried deep within the psyche. The false self emerges as a defensive barrier against maternal failure and acts as a bridge between the internal and external worlds of the child. This barrier protects the true self from "experiencing the threat of annihilation" (Ogden 1986, 143); however, at the same time, this can lead to distortions in psychological development. This distortion affects the creative potential of the child.

Winnicott (1960b) stated, "The False Self has one positive and very important function: to hide the True Self, which it does by compliance with environmental demands" (146–147). The defensive adaptation of the child to the environment by the creation of the false self is a way of preserving the integrity of the true self. Therefore, if the mother is intrusive, she impinges on the true self, forcing the development of a false self in her compliant child who is attuned to the wants or expectations of the mother. Winnicott further indicated that, "in extreme examples of False Self development, the True Self is so well hidden that spontaneity is not a feature in the infant's living experiences. Compliance is then the main feature, with imitation as a specialty" (147). When the degree of the rupture is minimal, "there may be some almost personal living through imitation, and it may even be possible for the child to act a special role, that of the True Self as it would be if it had existence" (147). During the period of relative dependence, children negotiate between inner psychic reality and external reality as they imagine both omnipotent control over their world and create symbols to 'bridge the gap' between internal and external experience.

Summary. The second stage of relative dependence helps define the separateness of infants from their mothers through the use of a transitional object. Transitional objects are referred to as the first 'not-me' object. Ogden (1986) depicted the transitional object as a symbol for separateness in unity or unity in separateness. The paradox is that the transitional object is at once the infant (i.e., an omnipotently created extension of himself) while also not the infant (i.e., an object discovered to be outside his omnipotent control). Winnicott (1960b) stated, "The baby creates the object, but the object was there waiting to be created" (221). It is the mother-object who sets the scene for discovery by the infant of the transitional object and, therefore, makes "I-ness" possible as the infant develops the capacity to "be alone in the presence of the mother" (Winnicott 1958, 30). The mother is, paradoxically, an absent object in the infant-generated potential space. This space is formless within which the infant can play alone in the presence of the absent mother.

Stage Three: Toward Independence

By the third stage of development, the healthy child is both separate from and part of the family, while moving out into the world, socializing with peers and going to school. This stage is particularly evident in the toddler and the child at puberty, but is also observed through adolescence. According to Winnicott (1963b),

> Adults must be expected to be continuing the process of growing and of growing up, since they do but seldom reach to full maturity. But once they have found a niche in society through work, and have perhaps married or have settled in some pattern that is a compromise between copying the parents and defiantly establishing a personal identity, once these developments have taken place, adult life can be said to have started, and the individuals one by one climb out of the area covered by this brief statement of growth in terms of dependence towards independence. (92)

Winnicott believed that the process of developing independence does not stop in childhood. Rather, it is a continual process. Although the adult has established a personal identity, the creative potential of the individual has no limits. As Winnicott stated, "Independence is never absolute. The healthy individual does not become isolated, but becomes related to the environment in such a way that the individual and the environment can be said to be interdependent" (84).

Conclusion

The process of emergence of self is a psychologically precarious movement through the series of developmental stages described—from absolute dependence to relative independence (Winnicott 1958). Each

stage, and especially the first two, is fraught with tension from opposing dialectical forces. The ability of the infant to navigate through these
stages intact is proportional to the devotion of the caretaker to the infant. Considering the three stages, it is clear that the most critical phase
of psychic development is the stage of absolute dependence—a period
of extreme vulnerability and a spawning ground for psychopathology.
Winnicott posited that psychotic illness emerges from this period when
the needs of the infant are not met by good-enough mothering. This
highly dependent phase of early infancy is critical for the psychological
formation of the infant because he is engaged in the complex process of
integration of the personality into a single unit. Self-perception is developed during this period and reinforced during the following stage of
relative dependence. The protagonists in the two stories examined in
this study exhibit trauma that can be traced to the first and second
stages of absolute and relative dependence.

CHAPTER 3

THE ENDURING CHILL

"The Enduring Chill" (O'Connor 1979a) explored the subsequent ramifications as an adult of sustained mother-infant merging that did not allow for separation. In this story, O'Connor examined the relationship between a mother and her son. At twenty-five years of age, Asbury Fox reluctantly returned home to the care of his mother because he believed he was dying. He left New York where he had journeyed to become a writer and returned to his Southern roots with a sense of profound sadness and failure at never reaching his goal. His mother—a widow in her sixties—single-handedly supported Asbury and his older sister, Mary George, after the death of her husband. She was a cold woman who efficiently oversaw the operation of the family dairy farm. Mrs. Fox referred to Asbury, and treated him, as though he was a small child, controlling his every move. Asbury responded as an angry, yet dependent child.

"The Enduring Chill" (O'Connor 1979a) characterizes how a rupture during the absolute-dependent stage of development can produce symptoms of dependence, lack of a sense of self, primitive omnipotence, and thwarted creativity in a child and in later adulthood. These symptoms are indicative of repetitive, early environmental impingement during the emergence of the infant ego. Applying the Winnicott (1964a) theory to this story, it can be hypothesized that external reality was thrust upon the infant Asbury prematurely, blurring differentiation between internal and external reality (O'Connor 1979a). He learned to *react* to an environment that did not appropriately respond, preventing him from resolving the developmental task of moving through the paradoxical stages required for going-on-being. Instead, Asbury the child was forced to respond to the needs of his mother, trapped in a symbiotically fused state. This rendered Asbury incapable of finding a

transitional space where the gradual sequence of separation and individuation could occur. As an adult, he felt the desire to be independent,
but was unable to achieve the state. The absence of a father further
complicated the scenario because Asbury had never experienced com-
pletion of the Oedipal struggle with the father that would free him from
the maternal bond.

Estrangement of Mother and Son

The train, in the opening sentence of "The Enduring Chill,"
wound its way through the metaphorically primitive terrain, deliver-
ing the twenty-five-year-old Asbury Fox to his mother who stood
waiting for him (O'Connor 1979a, 358). As mentioned earlier, Asbury
returned home because he believed he was dying, although he was not
actually suffering from a life-threatening illness. O'Connor wrote,
"He felt the end coming on for nearly four months . . . had become
entirely accustomed to the thought of death" (358). That first encounter between Asbury and Mrs. Fox, as he descended from the train,
implied a curious relationship. The short-lived smile on the face of
Mrs. Fox suddenly vanished and morphed into an expression of shock
as she witnessed the physical deterioration of her son. Asbury, however, was "pleased that she should see death in his face at once"
(357).

Eigen (1985) purported that the smile is "the home base of the human self, the felt criterion for what is most basically sensed as
emotionally right or wrong" (422). The smile on the face of Mrs. Fox
vanished as she observed the broken physical condition of her son;
however, Asbury interpreted her look in an emotionally reactive manner (O'Connor 1979a). It is hypothesized that a progression from the
passive to the active occurs in such interaction. In this case, Mrs. Fox
hoped to see in Asbury a mirror to herself, but she was met with decay
and impending death—precisely what Asbury desired her to see. Something ominous is implied by this encounter between mother and son,
something reminiscent of the description documented by Sterba (1940)
of a superstition of the Middle Ages. The wounds of a victim begin to
bleed at the approach of the murderer. Adding to this portentous scene
is the description of the phallic-like train that "glides silently away behind, [quickly becoming a] speck disappearing into the woods, [as
though] his last connection with a larger world were vanishing forever"
(O'Connor 1979a, 358).

To the reader, the opening sequence to the O'Connor (1979a) story offers a haunting image of mother and son exchanging odd reactions. Mrs. Fox says to Asbury, "It must have been cold up there. Why don't you take off your coat. It's not cold down here" (221). Asbury irritably responds, "You don't have to tell me what the temperature is! I'm old enough to know when I want to take my coat off" (221). This first verbal exchange between Mrs. Fox and Asbury provides a glimpse into the conflict between mother and son. There is a sense of icy coldness and doom in the "chill gray" sky that parallels the relationship between Mrs. Fox and Asbury. The woods are "black" and there is a "strange light" cast over the town. The expression on the face of Mrs. Fox is one "aghast," while Asbury stands "ill" and "bloodshot" (222).

A gloom of death hangs in the air, accentuating the pale and puffy face of Asbury. He becomes "entirely accustomed to the thought of death, but he had not become accustomed to the thought of death here" (O'Connor 1979a, 358). Asbury briefly imagines his return home as momentous and will magically reflect a major positive shift 'borrowed' from the previous trips home. He has a momentary illusion of greatness, "like some strange potentate from the East" whose arrival will introduce "his mother to reality" (223). This illusion is shattered, however, by a small but clear cry from Mrs. Fox that jars Asbury back to reality. His attention is drawn to the decaying town of Timborboro with its "flat roofs" and "one-story brick and wooden shacks" (223).

The eyes of Mrs. Fox peer at Asbury from a "thin spectacled face" as she says, "You don't look very well" (O'Connor 1979a, 223). Her eyes, distanced by her glasses, evoke a sense of reflection as Mrs. Fox looked at Asbury in a rather automated cold stare, rather than with the concern one would expect to observe in the face of a mother in such circumstances. Asbury is "pleased that she should see death in his face at once" (223). He enjoys shocking his mother, hoping to elicit some form of genuine recognition of his desperate state. Instead, Mrs. Fox observes Asbury with the "long clinical stare" (223); consequently, he shuts down like a rebelling teenager whose mother is intrusive, overbearing, and condescending. Mrs. Fox does not greet Asbury with a welcoming smile or hug. Instead, she notices how "his hair had receded tragically for a boy of twenty-five [bearing] down in a point that seemed to lengthen his nose" (223).

From the beginning of "The Enduring Chill" (O'Connor 1979a), relationships are strained between mother and son, and between brother and sister. Upon the arrival of Asbury at the train station, Mrs. Fox noted his "irritable expression that matched his tone of voice when he spoke to her" (223). In turn, Asbury observed his sister Mary George with "a revolted look of recognition" (225). He was only aware of his appearance by observing his mother's face and the "wide smile that disappeared as she caught sight of him . . . vanished so suddenly . . . that he realized for the first time that he must look as ill as he was" (223).

As the train vanished, Asbury's world began to shut down in a seemingly claustrophobic fashion (O'Connor 1979a). The first encounter between Asbury and his mother at the train station, caused Asbury to realize that nothing had changed. He found himself, once again, dependent upon her in a hostile manner, unable to escape her view of him as her 'little boy.' In a familiar pattern, Mrs. Fox was so engrossed in her own interpretation of her environment that she was incapable of understanding the feelings and needs of her son. As Winnicott (1970) espoused, symptoms of dependence, lack of a sense of self, and primitive omnipotence are indicators of repetitive maternal impingement during the early stage of absolute dependence.

Maternal Impingement

When applying the Winnicott (1970) theory to the "The Enduring Chill" (O'Connor 1979a), the predominant theme is impingement by a not-good-enough mother, with an accompanying Oedipal theme. It is difficult to imagine Mrs. Fox, glaring at Asbury from her "thin spectacled face" (223), capable of placing her own needs aside to devote herself to the protection and well-being of her infant. O'Connor described how she stared at Asbury with what appeared to be keen observation; however, what she seemed to actually see were her own cold and narrow distorted perceptions of life (as cited in Biedermann 1992). She rejected understanding for the following two possible reasons: (a) to maintain an image of Asbury as a dependent child/infant, or (b) she was incapable of an awareness of the suffering of others due to her narcissistic nature (O'Connor 1979a). Correspondingly, Asbury viewed himself as both her victim *and* self-object—passive, helpless, and impotent.

According to Winnicott (1963b), impingement is the result of the mother who "does . . . let her infant down" (86) by not adapting to the needs of her child. He is not referring merely to the 'instinctual' needs often referenced by Freud (as cited in Winnicott 1963b). Rather, as Winnicott explained, "A great deal of misconception has arisen out of the slowness of some to understand that an infant's needs are *not confined to instinct tensions,* important as they may be. *There is the whole of the infant's ego development that has its own needs*" (emphasis mine) (86). The ego needs to which Winnicott referred are incorporated in the maternal holding process involving both the physical and ego states of infants. A good-enough mother is aware of the needs of her child before the infant is aware of them, thus adapting herself to the needs of her baby. Failure of this adaptation by the mother "breaks up the going-on-being" (86) process, causing the infant to develop a pattern of reaction to impingements. Consequently, a "serious interference with the natural tendency that exists in the infant to become an integrated unit" is generated (86). By adaptation to the needs of the infant, the mother helps perpetuate the illusion of omnipotence for her child.

From the perspective of Winnicott, 'illusion' refers to the developmentally important experience for the infant of magical omnipotence or "self-completeness" (as cited in Useulli 1992, 279). There is no father to mediate this impasse between mother and son. The father is "needed by the child because of his positive qualities and the other things that distinguish the liveliness of his personality" (Winnicott 1968b, 115). Winnicott later adds, "It is . . . well known that a boy and his father do find themselves at times in a state of rivalry over mother. This need gives rise to no anxiety if mother and father are happy together" (118).

Asbury's father was not present, and it seemed apparent that Asbury had not passed the Oedipal complex (O'Connor 1979a). Without the presence of the father, the child is "dominated by an infantile part of the self, narcissistically identified with the mother" (Mancia 1993, 944). As such, he cannot tolerate separation and has no defined sense of self. In the case of Asbury, he must simultaneously defend against the threats of separation and suffocation (O'Connor 1979a). In reaction to the constant intrusiveness of his mother, Asbury finds himself in a perpetual state of irritability. For example, just as his return home represented a defense against separation, his emotional shutdown defended him against maternal impingement. These two forms of defense represent a classical paradox.

The following dialogue excerpt is not only an example of the intrusiveness of Mrs. Fox, but it also illustrates support of the nonsensical notion that separating from home/mother may cause death. While Asbury was napping, and contrary to his request, Mrs. Fox brought his past pediatrician, Dr. Block, into his room to examine him. Asbury awakened to the genitalia-like image of a "pink open-mouthed face hanging over him and from two large familiar ears" (O'Connor 1979a, 366). Infuriated, Asbury muttered to his mother, "Get him out of here," having told her earlier, "I am not seeing Block" (362, 366). To Dr. Block he said, "I didn't send for you" (366). However, his impotent complaints were ignored as Dr. Block remarked, "You sho do look bad, Azzberry" (366). Further, Dr. Block seemed to blame Asbury's condition on his move East when he stated, "You must have been on the bum up there. . . . Went up there *once* myself . . . and saw exactly how little they had and came straight back on home" (emphasis mine) (366). As Dr. Block's eyes seemingly drill into Asbury, he said, "I don't know when I've seen anybody your age look as sorry as you do" (O'Connor 1979a, 366). Dr. Block seemed to blame Asbury for his condition, asking, "What have you been doing to yourself?" Incensed, Asbury responded, "If I'd wanted a doctor, I'd have stayed up there where I could have got a good one" (366).

Asbury believed he was dying, and Dr. Block perceived Asbury's trip East as the source of his illness. Dr. Block drew his blood as Asbury, thinking there was nowhere to hide, lay passively with a "rigid outraged stare while the privacy of his blood was invaded by this idiot"(O'Connor 1979a, 367). He felt powerless against the clinical stares of both his mother and Dr. Block, standing there like a fused mother-father couple. His mind functioned with "terrible clarity" as he realized the impotent existence in store for him until he died (367).

Psyche-Soma Connection

In the situation described by O'Connor (1979a), there was no sense of what Winnicott (1958) referred to as "personalization" (6) as Asbury was startled from a nap by Dr. Block and his mother. It was as if there had been no protective membrane covering his skin as Dr. Block examined him and drew his blood (O'Connor 1979a). 'Personalization' is a term used to describe the infant at one year of age who is "living in the body" (Winnicott 1958, 6). When a child achieves personalization, he experiences a healthy relationship between the psyche and body, assuming "a reasonable degree of adaptation" by the mother since birth (6).

Asbury appears flat, passive, and does not have an integrated experience of mind and body (O'Connor 1979a). An example of this disconnection is observed in his reaction to illness. He imagines he is dying, based upon the fact that he feels physically ill. He does not go to a doctor to learn the facts. Instead, he keeps himself blind to external reality, existing in a feeling-reacting state, much like a newborn infant. Only when he observes the reaction of his mother to his appearance does Asbury make the connection that he must look as bad as he feels.

The example of intrusion by Dr. Block, initiated by the mother, demonstrates how Asbury was denied any physical or psychic boundaries (O'Connor 1979a). The presumption is that the impingement was a continuation of what he experienced as an infant from his environmental mother, making it difficult for him to make a psyche-soma association. Consequently, a sense of a "psychosomatic collusion" (Davis and Wallbridge 1981, 40)—the ability to synthesize the psyche-soma relationship—cannot develop. Winnicott (1960b) believed that the ability of the immature psyche to become connected to the body was an achievement linking "motor and sensory and functional experience" with the sense of self (45). Winnicott (1964b) also believed that, even when psychosomatic collusion has been established during the period of absolute dependence, there are periods when the psyche and body lose touch. He explained,

> There may be phases, in which it is not easy for the infant to come back into the body, for instance, when waking from deep sleep. Mothers know this, and they gradually wake an infant before lifting him or her, so as not to cause the tremendous screaming of panic which can be brought about by a change of position of the body at a time when the psyche is absent from it. Associated clinically with this absence of the psyche there may be pallor, times when the infant is sweating and perhaps very cold, and there may be vomiting. At this stage the mother can think her infant is dying, but by the time the doctor has arrived there has been so complete a return to normal health that the doctor is unable to understand why the mother was alarmed. (6)

The awakening experienced by Asbury leaves him disoriented (O'Connor 1979a). His mother not only intrudes upon his sleep, but she also invites Dr. Block to intrude upon the boundaries of his body. The difference between the description offered by Winnicott (1964b) of the infant being awakened from a deep sleep, and that offered by O'Connor of Asbury awakened from his nap, is that a sensitive mother would consider the welfare of her child first and would either allow him to sleep undisturbed or gently and slowly arouse him. Mrs. Fox imposed her own needs upon Asbury, abruptly intruding not only into the physical space of Asbury's room without knocking, but into his most vulnerable space—the psychic state of sleeping. Both of these intrusions support the impulsivity and lack of boundaries otherwise demonstrated by Mrs. Fox.

Mrs. Fox makes no accommodation for the needs of her son (O'Connor 1979a). Quite the contrary, he is sadistically jolted from a deep sleep by the voice of his mother and a doctor probing his body. There is no opportunity for Asbury to experience dominion over his own body and psyche with the intrusion while he is completely defenseless during slumber. If this account is an example of how Mrs. Fox treated Asbury during his early years of life, it could be concluded that she may well have neglected the provision of an initial trusting environment that would have encouraged an eventual sense of self for Asbury. It is more likely that Mrs. Fox chiseled an environment of her own liking, constantly and prematurely imposing it upon her infant, jarring him into an untimely awareness of his separateness and thereby causing him to react rather than to simply 'be'. As a result, Asbury does not comfortably inhabit his own body.

Dependence, Omnipotence, and the Good-Enough Mother

The infant who learns too early of his separateness cannot experience the shared illusion of omnipotence created by the good-enough mother (Useulli 1992). The infant learns that it is separate by the repeated impingement of the environmental mother, thereby discovering that it is dependent upon the mother for survival. The intrusive mother continuously reinforces this awareness and thus maintains the dependency of the infant upon her. For example, Asbury experienced futility in attempting to separate from Mrs. Fox (O'Connor 1979a). No requisite bridge exists between fantasy and reality that facilitates development. She made Asbury dependent upon her to the extent where he was incapable of separation. His feeble protests went unheard.

The futility of the attempts made by Asbury to individuate became obvious as his condition deteriorated. His mother began to insist that, in the middle of the day, he get out and sit on the porch and enjoy the view (O'Connor 1979a). The view to which she referred was framed by trees and barbed wire that intended to keep the cows enclosed; however, it seemed to serve Mrs. Fox better in keeping Asbury confined, forcing him to listen to her talk of the "intimate functions" of cows with "their mastitis and their screwworms and their abortions" (367). Female trappings in the form of his mother, sister, and cows surrounded Asbury.

Asbury equated himself to the 'Negroes' who worked for his mother—those people under her control. Yet, somehow, Asbury felt emotionally beneath them, for "they know how to look after themselves," and he did not (O'Connor 1979a, 368). The Negroes were free, and he was not. The Negroes working for Mrs. Fox simply accepted and followed her rules while maintaining their integrity. They knew their position, yet maintained their self-sufficiency. Asbury attempted to free himself by rejecting those things important to his mother, such as the land, and coveting those things distasteful to her such as fleeing East. He described his trip East as an education and a way to "escape the slave's atmosphere of home . . . to find freedom, to liberate my imagination, to take it like a hawk from its cage and set it 'whirling off into the widening gyre' (Yeats) and what did I find? I was incapable of flight" (363). Asbury referred to a loss of freedom and the burden of his internalized slavery. Winnicott (1966d) stated, "The subject of freedom has already been introduced when I refer to the environmental factor rendering creativity useless or destroying it in an individual by producing a state of hopelessness. This is the subject of freedom in terms of the lack of and the cruelty that is involved in either physical restraint or in the annihilation of an individual's personal existence by dominance" (228). An example of the intrusion by Mrs. Fox was her "little cry," which interrupted the fantasy entertained by Asbury at the beginning of the story where he imagines a majestic return home (O'Connor 1979a, 357). She then demands that Asbury remove his coat. Perhaps the most imposing intrusion by Mrs. Fox is her subsequent insistence that Asbury fulfill her own desire to become a writer by commanding that *he* write a novel about the South that would surpass *Gone With the Wind*.

Creativity Thwarted

In "The Enduring Chill," Asbury had the desire to write, but admitted failure as a writer. He stated, "I have not talent. I can't create" (O'Connor 1979a, 364). In the eyes of his sister, he had no writing gift, and she tried to persuade her mother of this fact. O'Connor wrote, "Mary George had said that if Asbury had had any talent, he would by now have published something" (363). Mrs. Fox clung to the belief that Asbury "might be writing a very *long* book" (emphasis mine) (363). Asbury, who believed his sister "posed as an intellectual but that her I.Q. couldn't be over 75," admitted, "I have nothing but desire" to write (364). Consequently, between talent and desire, he could only create "lifeless novels," "prosy poems," and "sketchy short stories" (365). As Asbury continued to lament over the immobility of his writing, he described his own psychic turmoil by stating, "I have no imagination" (364).

Possessing only the longing to be truly creative, Asbury faulted his mother as he asked, "Why didn't you kill that too?" (O'Connor 1979a, 364). In despair, he lamented in a grandiose manner with a subsequent query of "Woman, why did you pinion me?" (364), self-consciously echoing Jesus who, nailed to the cross, cried out to his Father, "Why hast thou forsaken me?" Asbury blamed the suppression by his mother for his lack of imagination. As O'Connor described it, "Her way had simply been the air he breathed and when at last he had found other air, he couldn't survive in it" (365).

Asbury believed his mother to be incapable of seeing the "significance . . . of all she had done to him. [He equated himself to] some bird [his mother] had domesticated, sitting huffy in its pen, refusing to come out" (O'Connor 1979a, 364). This image is quite contrary to that of the hawk Asbury so desperately desired to set free. There is no space to play in Asbury's world because the environment is untrustworthy. According to Winnicott (1971b), "It is creative appreciation more than anything else that makes the individual feel that life is worth living. Contrasted with this is a relationship to external reality which is one of *compliance*, the world and its details being recognized but only as something to be fitted in with or demanding adaptation. Compliance carries with it a sense of futility for the individual and is associated with the idea that nothing matters and that life is not worth living" (emphasis mine) (65).

Mrs. Fox continuously projected her own needs upon Asbury, confining her son to a level of excessive instinctual arousal (i.e., 'fight or flight') where the luxury of play is impossible because playing requires potential space. Asbury craved liberation, but was trapped by fear of separation. He had gone East to liberate himself from the emotional clutches of his mother, to gain an education, and to become a writer; however, he was so emotionally dominated by his mother, he was unable to effectuate separation. Therefore, any threat of imagination is replaced by feeble desire.

Writing is an escape or a means of establishing an "autarchic fantasy" (Wormhoudt 1949, 57). It is regression to an oral level without the need for mother's milk. Language then becomes "words-milk" (57), replacing the breast and thereby excluding the mother. However, Asbury cannot write and, therefore, cannot exclude his mother (O'Connor 1979a). Mrs. Fox stifles any hope of creativity in Asbury by her incessant demands for compliance and dependence. Asbury has the desire for nourishment, but the muse is dry. His attempts at writing are not fluid as milk, but rather, they curdle into unmovable clots. Asbury subsequently views himself as a failure and destroys all of his writing endeavors with the exception of one letter.

The Letter

The single remaining letter written by Asbury is the culmination of his life experience and pressed to paper in precious lifeblood (O'Connor 1979a). It is certainly not authored by a master artist in the literal sense because he did not study nor practice his wordsmithery as a skilled artisan. His words are the utterances of a broken spirit preserved within an envelope, never to be read nor understood. This missive, neatly containing his anger, was to be delivered to his mother upon his death. It was the unstated wish of Asbury to kill his mother through this letter, a parallel act to his own death, which he attributed to her.

The letter becomes a poisonous documentation of the toxic nature of the mothering extended by Mrs. Fox to her son (O'Connor 1979a). Consequently, Asbury can be compared to the mythical nymph Echo, whom Hera deprives of original speech and thought (Biedermann 1992). As creative possibilities fade for Asbury, as a direct result of the intervention by his mother, he is able to still grasp the last word through his letter (O'Connor 1979a). Asbury imagines that, by reading the letter, his mother will "at least begin to sense his tragedy and her part of it" (364). He fantasizes the impact the legacy of his letter will have on his mother. O'Connor commented that "this would be the only thing of value he had to leave her" (364).

Asbury equated the importance of the letter to his mother to that of the letter "Kafka had addressed to his father" (O'Connor 1979a, 364) and, in this way, he narcissistically enlarged his importance in his own mind. His letter became his 'art'—a tribute to the failed mothering of Mrs. Fox. It is Asbury's aim to leave her with an "enduring chill" (365), the same kind of haunting, cold feeling she brought to his own experience—a feeling that lingered like his fever. "It'll keep coming back but it won't kill [her]" (381). He wanted to get into her bones, to cause her to ache with the same kind of impotent desire he experienced. However, with the knowledge that he was indeed not at death's door, Asbury was forced to take back his letter, forfeiting the last word. The opportunity to 'nourish' Mrs. Fox with his thoughts, or fill her with the 'enduring chill' she imparted to him was lost.

Asbury was engaged in a psychological war with his mother. He used impotent ploys to irritate her as he encouraged the Negro employees to smoke with him in the creamery, thereby tainting or poisoning the milk. Mrs. Fox refused to blame Asbury, even though he admitted it was his fault. The experience of upsetting his mother "had so exhilarated him that he had been determined to repeat it in some other way" (O'Connor 1979, 369). He employed passive-aggressive techniques against her to gain personal satisfaction. As he demanded that a Jesuit priest be summoned for intellectual stimulation, his face brightened at the prospect of further shocking and irritating his mother in his attempt "to play both ends against the middle" (371). He cajoled his mother into granting his wish using the plea of impending death. "I'm dying, and I haven't asked you to do but one thing and you refuse me that" (372).

Priest as Father

The priest was a "massive old man" who, with a "loud" voice, "plowed straight across [Asbury's] room" and sat down beside the bed. He announced himself as "Father Finn from Purgatory" (O'Connor 1979a, 374–375). He was uneducated and "blind in one eye and deaf in one ear" (375). The priest was the epitome of the relationship between Asbury and Mrs. Fox because he focused on one idea to the exclusion of everything else. He also belied the notion Asbury held of priests as "worldly," cynical, and well-educated, which Asbury adopted through his memory of the aloof priest, Ignatius Vogle, S. J., whom he had met at a Buddhist lecture (371).

Father Finn, in response to questioning posed by Asbury, was dogmatically interested only in religious inquiry, as evidenced in his first query to Asbury asking, "Do you say your morning and night prayers?" (O'Connor 1979, 375). Asbury attempted to engage the priest in an intellectual discussion by stating, "The myth of the dying god has always fascinated me," to which the priest responded, "How do you expect to meet God's face when you've never spoken to Him?" (375–376), which is a common parallel used in mythic criticism—comparing Christ to other gods such as Attis, Adonis, Osiris, or Baldur. However, in this instance, Father Finn ignored Asbury's comment—possibly due to a lack of understanding—and again concretely addressed the issue of divine forgiveness.

Asbury consciously used the priest as a ploy as he hid behind his false-self aura of an intellectual to irritate his mother (O'Connor 1979a). Subconsciously, Asbury had summoned a priest to service as a father substitute to intercede between Asbury and his mother in a type of Oedipal intervention. In his mind, he acknowledged he was trapped and fully dominated by his mother. His only hope was male intervention. The priest, however, with his "terrible" good eye, pinned Asbury to the bed with religious dogma (377). He began with "Do you want your soul to suffer eternal damnation? Do you want to suffer the most terrible pain, greater than fire, the pain of loss? Do you want to suffer the pain of loss for all eternity?" (377). Ironically, Asbury had already felt this form of pain in life. When the priest turned to loud criticisms of Asbury as a "lazy, ignorant conceited youth," Mrs. Fox then became the intercessor as she informed the priest that Asbury was simply a "poor sick boy" (377). The priest stated the truth to Mrs. Fox: "You have neglected your duty as his mother"; however, he added, "I should think you would have taught him to say his daily prayers" (377). Consequently, he addressed her failure to educate Asbury properly in matters of the church while neglecting her true failure as a good-enough mother. Father Finn did not understand that the behavior demonstrated by Asbury was in reaction to the impinging nature of Mrs. Fox.

To obtain some form of nurturance, Asbury must assume a childlike role in relationship to Mrs. Fox (O'Connor 1979a). This regressed state is primitive in nature, and his childish attempts to connect with his mother become regressions to an oral level with a need for the warmth of milk from a good-enough mother. For example, to spite orders given from Mrs. Fox, he steals a drink from the container of raw, warm, unpasteurized milk with full knowledge of the potential risk of undulant fever. However, instead of successfully inducing anger in his mother, his attempts 'backfire'. The milk poisons Asbury. To paraphrase Winnicott (1957), this milk flows like excrement. The less the breast is available, the greater the desire, and desire leads to knowledge of the "presence of the absence" (Eigen 1986, 64). Like the intricate fruit carved into the ornate wooden headboard of Asbury's bed (O'Connor 1979a), the illusion is bountiful, but the reality is barren.

Winnicott (1948) referred to Shakespeare's Juliet in her infancy. He mentioned the fact that Juliet's mother, who was thirteen years of age at the time, relinquished care of her daughter to a wet nurse of fourteen who had just lost a child. The nurse adored Juliet and did not wean her until she was three. When she did wean her, it was with "bitter alves" in an "indirect way" (33). Winnicott explained,

> It seems to me that Shakespeare was trying to show why Juliet had to have the split in her nature. The compliance to her mother and everybody is all right for this other thing, the extreme of romanticism, whereby the impossible is going to happen. She is going to have all the feelings of love in relation to somebody who is coming along, something, which is actually doomed to end in death and actual poisoning. A great deal made of the poisoning being a breast experience, being good because it is bad [irony]. . . . He was describing somebody without any bridges between the inner world and external reality. (33)

This description of Juliet is reminiscent of Asbury who, on one hand, complies with the demands of his mother, yet acts out a symbolic poisoning at his mother's breast through the literal poisoning of himself when drinking tainted milk (O'Connor 1979a). He drinks the raw, unpasteurized milk with full knowledge that he risks potential infection—a gamble he ultimately loses. In this sense, two things then become compartmentalized for Asbury—loving (i.e., including aggressive/destructive impulses) and complying. The "taking of what was [not] given" is another aspect at work (22). The cows' milk and the mother's milk become indistinguishable. Winnicott (1967a) explained, "The vast majority of difficulties in infant feeding have nothing to do with infection or with the biochemical unsuitability of the milk. They have to do with the immense problem that every mother has in adapting to the needs of baby" (40). Mrs. Fox was a demanding woman who may have well expected Asbury, as an infant, to comply to *her* needs, if her later behavior toward the adult Asbury is any indication (O'Connor 1979a).

The breast, in the Lacanian sense, is always a signifier of desire "with a bad quarter" (Weatherhill 1994, 83–89). Asbury had the desire for nourishment, but the teats of the cow—the O'Connor (1979a) symbol for the mother—are defective. They have mastitis, they produce toxic milk, or they are dry. Mrs. Fox continuously emphasizes the defects in the cows that prevent their ability to produce milk. Her comments are a constant admonition that her needs have not been met by Asbury. They also serve to remind Asbury of his own unmet needs. Consequently, when Mrs. Fox drove up the path to the house upon bringing Asbury home from the train station, she stopped abruptly when she spotted a cow. When she cried out almost hysterically, "They haven't been attending to her . . . look at that bag," she seemed to be addressing her own abandonment (362). Asbury turned his head away, begging to go home, but was faced with yet another cow—"a small walleyed Guernsey watching him steadily as if she sensed some bond between them" (362). Everywhere Asbury affixed his gaze, he was reminded of failure and loss. There was nowhere to hide, and any aggressive thoughts Asbury had toward his mother were potentially dangerous and always backfired, as demonstrated when he attempted to get close to his mother by 'helping' in the dairy and, in return, was kicked by a cow.

Asbury returned home to the same 'dry' atmosphere that reminded him of his failed maternal bond (O'Connor 1979a; Trad 1991). The aggression demonstrated by Mrs. Fox toward Asbury for leaving is clearly played out as she continued to focus on the cows (O'Connor 1979a). On the surface, it appeared that she was attempting to neutralize her aggression as she focused it onto the care of the cows; however, this behavior was actually a sadistic reminder to Asbury of how, when he leaves, something 'dries up' between them. Cruelly, it seemed that his mother cared more for the cows than for Asbury. It was only natural, therefore, that the sight of the cows upset him when he could look in no direction without seeing one. They were constant reminders of the tenuous nature of the maternal bond. Even the androgynous sister, Mary George, added to the consternation Asbury felt when she remarked in a harsh, nasal voice, "How utterly, utterly" (362), playing on the word 'udder'.

Trad (1991) also described the destructive behavior of mothers toward infants attempting to separate. Such mothers personalize the behavior of these infants and retaliate in kind. They often become resentful of the infant whose head is turned away from their breast and react with punishment. When the hungry infant cries, a mother such as this can often withhold the breast. By doing this, she unconsciously and symbolically spoils her breast milk so that the ungrateful infant will be deprived of nourishment and subsequently starve.

Home: Entrapment, Fusion, and Emotional Infanticide

Mary George analogized the return home of her brother to "the artist [arriving] at the gas chamber" (O'Connor 1979a, 363). The allusion to the Holocaust seemed appropriate. Asbury "[moved] toward the house as if in a daze," like being led to a death chamber (364). He returned home on a train—also parallel to the Jews transported by train to death camps. He is not confined to a cattle car, as the Jews were; he traveled in coach. However, from the train station, he was transported home—to the family dairy farm—in the stifling close atmosphere of his mother's car. On the path leading to the house, Asbury felt enveloped by cows on either side of the road. Mrs. Fox, aware only that she had her son back home, drove the car into a flock of screaming guineas as she chimed a verse of an old nursery rhyme: "Home again, home again, jiggity jig" (363).

According to Mrs. Fox, there are those that would give their "eyeteeth" to have her home (O'Connor 1979a, 362). This image is both aggressive and primitive as eyeteeth are the incisors also known as canine teeth used to rip meat. Therefore, to have Mrs. Fox home, the submissive act of relinquishing aggressive potential is implied. Winnicott (1965) stated,

> In health a large proportion of the aggressive potential becomes fused in with the infant's instinctual experiences, and with the pattern of the individual infant's

relationships. Good-enough environmental conditions are necessary for this development to take place. In ill health only a small proportion of the aggressive potential becomes fused in with the erotic life, and the infant is then burdened with impulses that make no sense. These eventually lead to destructiveness in the relationship to objects, or, worse, form the basis of activity that is entirely senseless. (12)

In the submission of his aggressive potential, time seemed to stop or slow down for Asbury (O'Connor 1979a). Faces and emotions seemed vague or frozen, as though carved into the environment. Asbury, for example, has a "wooden resigned expression" and a "white wooden face" (365). Mary George displayed a "revolted look of recognition" and said to Asbury, "If I looked as bad as you, I'd go to the hospital" (365). Goetz "[takes] the news of Asbury's approaching end with a calm indifference" (359). A "wall-eyed guernsey [stares at Asbury] as if she sensed some bond between them" (362). A stain on the ceiling menacingly stared down at Asbury like a "fierce bird with spread wings" (365), and Dr. Block stared at Asbury with "two cold clinical nickel-colored eyes, [a] drill-like gaze [and a] gaze [that] seemed to reach down like a steel pin and hold whatever it was until the life was out of it" (381); Father Finn had focused his one good eye sharply on Asbury.

As mentioned earlier, according to Mary George, the house belonging to Mrs. Fox equated to a gas chamber for Asbury who felt as confined as a bird in a cage. When Mary George inquired, "What's wrong with [Asbury]?" Mrs. Fox responded, "There's the house" (O'Connor 1979a, 362). The question posed by Mary George caused anxiety in Mrs. Fox. She did not wish to discuss Asbury's illness because it was too disturbing to her. Instead, she focused her attention on the house, which "rose on the crest of the hill—a white two-story farmhouse with a wide porch and pleasant columns" (362). The description is voluptuously feminine, inviting, and sensuous. Mrs. Fox could hardly wait to get Asbury inside. Once in his bedroom, Asbury observed the familiar water stain on the faded gray wall above his bed. The image from his childhood emerged, resembling a "fierce bird with spread wings" and an icicle in its beak (365). This image "had always irritated him and sometimes had frightened him. He often had the illu-

sion that the image was in motion and about to descend mysteriously
and set the icicle on his head" (366).

Although there are no overt sexual overtones in "The Enduring
Chill" (O'Connor 1979a), sensuality is prevalent in the descriptions
embedded in the story. Asbury suffered from undulant fever, a disease
that can, ironically, mimic an early environmental failure and is caused
from drinking unpasteurized cow milk. This illness is related to
'bangs', a similar disease prevalent in cows. The terms 'undulant' and
bangs present libidinous connotations. Undulant is a voluptuous sound-
ing, three-syllable word. When uttered, it thrusts the tongue forward
and backward while pursing the lips together, similar to the fusion of
the aggressive and erotic aspects of coitus where movements rise and
fall, heave, swell, and ripple. More simply, undulant also recalls the
sea—a feminine symbol referring to the movement of waves. The slang
use of the term bang is a more vulgar and less sensual version of the
word undulate.

The fever endured by Asbury presented a type of 'spend passion.' It "gradually [slackened] his energy and [caused] vague
inconsistent aches and headaches," as though he had been drained or
consumed (O'Connor 1979a, 358). Asbury succumbed to a fever
with sexual implications linked to unnatural maternal fusion, which
mimicked repressed incestuous desire. In this case, fever becomes
both a sexual Oedipal fire and an intellectual Promethean fire or a
'Prometheus complex', where "all those tendencies [sexual and in-
tellectual] impel us *to know* as much as our fathers, more than our
fathers, as much as our teachers, [and] more than our teachers" (emphasis mine) (Bachelard 1964, 12). This knowledge, however, has
its price. According to Bachelard, "Never has the Oedipus complex
been better and more completely revealed: if you lack fire, this burn-
ing failure will gnaw at your heart, the fire will remain within you. If
you produce fire, the sphinx itself will consume you. Love is but a
fire that is to be transmitted. Fire is but a love whose secret is to be
detected" (24). The fever also becomes a contradiction. "It can go
back down into the substance and hide there, latent and pent-up, like
hate and vengeance" (7). Asbury's (O'Connor 1979a) fever became
the "objective phenomenon of an inner rage, of a hand which has
become irritable" (Bachelard 1964, 36).

In the Name of the Father

Asbury carries the name of his father, but speaks his mother's tongue because his father died when he was five years of age (O'Connor 1979a). Consequently, Asbury consistently searches for idealized father figures, finding one in the emotionally reserved Father Vogel. 'Vogel' in German means 'bird'—an important symbol in "The Enduring Chill" due to Asbury's illusion of the stain on the wall above his bed as a bird hovering menacingly above him. Asbury referred to his biological father as "the old man who, he felt sure, had been one of the courthouse gang, a rural worthy with a dirty finger in every pie" (364). He learns about his father by reading his correspondence and is "appalled by its stupidity" (361).

According to Mrs. Fox, her husband "was a lawyer and business-man and farmer and politician all rolled into one and had his feet on the ground. . . . [He had] gone to a one-room schoolhouse through the 8th grade and he could do anything" (O'Connor 1979a, 361). Asbury seemed enraged at his father for dying and leaving him alone with his mother. Yet, he created a personal myth that depicted his father as a scoundrel, telling others his death was "a great blessing" to avoid ex-periencing the enormous sense of loss (364). Consequently, he remained enmeshed with Mrs. Fox without the benefit of fatherly inter-vention. He was left without the knowledge gained from experiencing and surviving the "dream of violent overthrow" encountered in the Oedipus complex where "identification with the father" occurs (Winni-cott 1965, 92). According to Winnicott, "The Oedipus complex comes as a relief, since in the triangular situation the boy can retain the love of the mother with the idea of the father in the way. . . . Where only the child and the mother are concerned, there are only two alternatives, to be swallowed up or to break free" (92). Thus, without the presence of the father, Mrs. Fox dominated Asbury (O'Connor 1979a).

Mrs. Fox became the "air [Asbury] breathes" (O'Connor 1979a, 365). Any aggression felt by Asbury was potentially destructive. Con-sequently, the aggression demonstrated was either played out in impotent devices intended to annoy his mother, such as attempting to corrupt the hired help, or was deflected into space such as the bird stain above his bed that became a dangerous potential for retribution. The bird stain is a complex projection of both the aggression and terror of Asbury, symbolizing a link between maternal deprivation and narcissis-tic rage. Further, the bird symbolized a childish construction of the

Oedipal father. It became apparent that Asbury had not yet experienced, before latency, a "full-blooded Oedipus complex . . . of the two main positions in the triangular relationship with the two parents" (Winnicott 1965, 80). Within this triangular experience of the Oedipal complex, "the child learns experientially the meaning of interpersonal relationships" (145). Because Asbury (O'Connor 1979a) had not experienced the Oedipal complex, he did not have "organized ways of warding off distress or of accepting and tolerating the conflicts" (Winnicott 1965, 80). Therefore, he experienced overwhelming anxiety (O'Connor 1979a).

According to Winnicott (1958), "Anxiety concerns the conflict, largely in the unconscious, between love and hate" (103). One way in which Asbury expresses anxiety is by projections, such as the bird stain, created to defend against intolerable distress (O'Connor 1979a). According to Winnicott (1968a), "If the father dies this is significant, and when exactly in the baby's life he dies, and there is a great deal too to be taken into account that has to do with the imago of the father in the mother's inner reality and its fate there" (242). From the negative description Asbury portrayed of his father, it appeared that the imago Mrs. Fox held for his father was designed to shut Mr. Fox out to allow her exclusivity with Asbury, resulting in a symbiotic merging of mother and son (O'Connor 1979a). In a healthy triangular relationship among mother, father, and child, the father's role as head male in the family, and mate of the mother, is wielded, thereby thwarting the rivalrous intentions of the son. Without relational parameters enforced by the father, the son is not encouraged to separate from the mother. Additionally, with a mother who encourages fusion, the child becomes a replacement for the father (Mancia 1993).

In the case of Asbury, the father seemed to have played a minimal to nonexistent role in helping Asbury separate from his mother (O'Connor 1979a). Whether it was unavailability or the barrier of Mrs. Fox between the father and son, Asbury was unable to become a separate unit. Although he attempted to venture from home by traveling East in his quest to independently obtain an education and become a writer, he could not stay away. O'Connor wrote, "Ever since he had first gone away to college, he had come back every time with nothing but the necessities for a two-week stay and with a wooden resigned expression that said he was prepared to endure the visit for *exactly fourteen days*" (emphasis mine) (358).

The word 'wooden' is frequently referred to throughout "The En-during Chill" (O'Connor 1979a) and seems important when contrasted to the concept of authenticity posited by Winnicott (1968b). The flights from the maternal home, exemplified in the preceding O'Connor (1979a) quote, are similar to those of Herman Melville, who, at seven-teen, fled from home to escape a "melancholy situation" (Rosenheim 1940, 2). Melville's mother, as was the case with Mrs. Fox (O'Connor 1979a), is described as "cold, haughty, formal, proper, putting the high-est premium upon appearance" (Rosenheim 1940, 2). Melville, as was Asbury, is described as a "pale, thin and dejected" youngster who was "backward in speech [and] slow in comprehension" (2). Unlike Asbury (O'Connor 1979a), however, Melville (Rosenheim 1940) understood "men and things both solid and profound and [was] of an amiable dis-position" (2). Melville's father, a somewhat unsuccessful sailor, died when Melville was thirteen; hence, he had the presence of a male figure past the Oedipal stage.

Asbury existed in a female-dominated environment in which the absence of male energy was striking. The women were more masculine than the men, as alluded to in the description of Dr. Block as a great big baby with his "pink open-mouthed face" (O'Connor 1979a, 366). Only the two hired Negroes, who were under the tight control of Mrs. Fox, represent a masculine presence. In contrast to the hired help are the two Jesuit priests and Dr. Block, all of whom suggest the sexual impotence of the father, and then there is Mary George—a female with a half-masculine name, and also a name that implies sexual ambiguity.

Mary George, an elementary school principal, wore Girl Scout shoes; was a larger, more masculine version of Asbury and possessed a more masculine, pragmatic attitude. At one point, Mary George said to Mrs. Fox, "Grow up, Mamma. . . . I've told you [once] and I tell you again: what's wrong with [Asbury] is purely psychosomatic" (373). Mary George advised that Asbury is not, has never been, and never will be a writer. In her opinion, all he needed was a couple of shock treat-ments to startle him back to reality. Reality, for Asbury, was a painful circumstance to avoid at all costs. The magnitude of this distress was expressed in one of his dreams.

The Dream within a Dream

Asbury experienced a pivotal dream in two parts, both of which ex-posed a sense of maternal/paternal rejection (O'Connor 1979a). The dream serves as a kind of poem of the unconscious as it portrays the diseased body of Asbury as his earthly house, and the fever as the fire that was destroying it (Jung 1964; O'Connor 1979a). In the first part of the dream, Asbury witnessed the "peaceful spot in the family burying ground where he would soon lie" (O'Connor 1979a, 374). He watched as his body was slowly "carried" by "indistinct mourners" on a bier across a dam to be laid in a shallow grave (368). The juxtaposition of the words 'indistinct' and 'mourners' established a peculiar tension. 'Indistinct' implies out of focus, obscure, or even unnoticeable, in the same manner that Asbury felt unseen in his dream. The word 'mourners' describes individuals engaged in grieving and weeping; however, these are unknown mourners with whom Asbury had no connections. Only their vague presence was observed with no sense of emotion. The "china blue sky" (368) glared down as Mrs. Fox and Mary George watched the processional "without interest from their chairs on the porch" (374). Asbury observed the reflection of the entire display "upside down in the pond" (374). His corpse seemed to be resting directly on the bier without the containment of a coffin as it was transported to its shallow resting place on a hillside.

In poetry, hills and mountains are often breast symbols. In Greek poetry, the muses lived on mountains and "guarded sacred springs. . . . Liquid from these springs . . . inspired the poets," supporting the theory that poetry stems from the oral level of unconsciousness (Wormhoudt 1949, 57). Consequently, the muses are pregenital mother symbols. In the dream experienced by Asbury in "The Enduring Chill," Mrs. Fox and Mary George were observing, but not musing, as the funeral procession passed before them (O'Connor 1979a). Although there was a reflection in the water below the dam, there was nothing sacred there. Water is a female substance in its elemental state (Bachelard 1964).

The grave was shallow and the mountain was reduced to a hill. Following the bier was a "lean, dark figure in a Roman collar" (O'Connor 1979a, 374). This ominous presence had a "mysteriously saturnine face in which there was a subtle blend of asceticism and corruption" (374). This frightening image, which is not at all subtle, lurked behind the procession, invoking an image resembling the description Asbury used for his father. The symbolism of the Jesuit priests—Father Vogel and Father Finn—to whom Asbury looked to as father figures, is also evident. Both are sexless. Asbury desired to be like Father Vogel—cold, uninvolved, and impervious. However, his outcome was frustration with Father Finn who was a 'damaged' priest and not too bright, but clear and confident on the concept of religion. Because Asbury does not know his father, he possessed no clear knowledge of the role of a father. Therefore, he remained confused about men in general and their roles.

The breast and phallus confusion experienced by Asbury is represented in the dream description of the Jesuit standing under a dead tree smoking a cigarette while meditating (O'Connor 1979a). This image is similar to the experience of Asbury smoking cigarettes in the dairy, intentionally tainting the milk of his mother's cows. The sexual inferences of smoking a cigarette have a convoluted quality. On one end of the spectrum, it was as though Asbury was sucking on the breast as he figuratively unites with the two dark figures representing the hired help, via the fire from the cigarette, to taint the milk. The cigarette was lit by fire, and fire is created by friction. The smoke from the cigarette penetrated the milk. On the other end of the spectrum, the cigarette assumed a phallic quality, as though it was being drained of semen/smoke, thereby becoming impotent.

Asbury (O'Connor 1979a) desired nourishment from his mother, but contracted undulant fever instead—a clear image of poisonous maternity. Asbury also needed his father to intervene; however, his real father was dead and his idealized 'fathers' were impotent. The priest smoked a cigarette by a dead tree. The smoke from that cigarette was from "unnatural" feminine fire "which corrupts the chemical compound and which first has the power of dissolving that which nature had strongly joined together" (Bachelard 1964, 52). Asbury's denial of the significance of his natural father, which accompanies the idealization of pregenital modes of sexual relationships, became unleashed in the dream (O'Connor 1979a).

The first part of the dream experienced by Asbury was vague and out of focus (O'Connor 1979a). The scene evoked a deep sense of isolation and disconnection. The sky glared, mother and sister observed without interest, and things were viewed upside down as though through the internal mechanizations of a camera lens. Looking directly at any object is potentially dangerous. When Asbury peered into a mirror, he saw a "pale, broken face" (363) and gaped at the world with a "wooden resigned expression" (358). The second part of the dream focused on the brightness of the moon. The moon, in most cultures, is a female symbol, combining death and rebirth (Biedermann 1992, 224). Consequently, this portion of the dream had a resurrection motif as As-

bury was aware of a presence bending over him (O'Connor 1979a).
This segment was both regressed and hopeful, as the infant Asbury felt
"a gentle warmth on his cold face" (374). Responding to that warmth,
Asbury opened his eyes and sat up, believing 'art' had come "to wake
him" (374) like the "gentle heat [that] is at the source of the conscious-
ness of happiness" (Bachelard 1964, 36). 'Art', in this context, is
Asbury's desire for nourishment provided by a tender mother
(O'Connor 1979a).

Mrs. Fox was a frustrated artist (O'Connor 1979a). Since Asbury
was a narcissistic extension of Mrs. Fox, it was *she* who was vicariously the artist, fashioning Asbury into an artifice of her own needs and
desires. This impingement was exemplified when Mrs. Fox tried to
contain Asbury in his room when she informed him his trip home was
permanent. "Wonderful! . . . You can have a little studio in our room
and in the mornings you can write plays and in the afternoons you can
help in the dairy" (365). Mrs. Fox held firmly to the delusion that Asbury was also going to write the great American novel, and thereby
make *her* important. What she did not understand was that Asbury
would never become an artist because she did not allow his creative
potential to develop. An unconscious disappointment and rage looms
throughout the story, as if Mrs. Fox must be protected from it.

In the dream, as in reality, cows surround Asbury (O'Connor
1979a). In folklore, there is an association between the milk of a cow
and moonlight. In the Norse myth of creation, the cow Audumla is the
original creature on earth and licked the first man into existence out of
salty blocks of ice (Biedermann 1992). As Asbury lay in the pasture,
'Art,'—a large, "violently spotted" cow—licked his head "like a block
of salt" (O'Connor 1979a, 374). This image is reminiscent of the biblical wife of Lot who was turned into a pillar of salt for looking back at
Sodom and Gomorrah (Gen. 19:1–29 NKJV). In the dream, Asbury
looks toward his mother's house, just as Lot's wife turned to see the
destruction of her village (Gen. 19:1–29 NKJV; O'Connor 1979a).
Looking leads to misfortune. This image demonstrates how paralyzed
Asbury was in relation to his mother (O'Connor 1979a).

Asbury's dream represents confusion over the concepts of warmth
and nurturance (O'Connor 1979a). Asbury wanted these qualities in his
own life so desperately that he observed them in his dream. His head,
which at first, felt the warmth of the cow's tongue as a mother's warm
hand, became a block of salt when he opened his eyes and saw what

was really happening. Asbury did not observe a kindly mother. The cow (i.e., mother) in this situation became a trickster, just as the name 'Fox' implies. Mrs. Fox seduced Asbury with seeming warmth, but her hidden aggression made a slave of her son. These deceits, reflected in the dream, stole the life force from Asbury as he succumbed to them (Biedermann 1992; O'Connor 1979a). Consequently, Asbury experienced confusion between the dream state (i.e., desire) and reality. This uncertainty is likened to the "geographical confusion" described by Mancia (1993, 945), which equates to the inability to distinguish body parts. This is comparable to the perplexing images in the mind of an infant that could lead to the inability to differentiate between sperm and milk.

Literal confusion between semen and breast milk has been observed within other cultures. Reisner (1994), in a comparison study of male schizophrenics and normal Zambia males in new Guinea, reported that, in some instances, schizophrenics confuse semen with milk and fear being "drained" during intercourse (63). For some schizophrenics, the draining fantasy occurs when the geographical boundaries between mother and infant are confused in combination with early trauma. Developmental frustration of the male child by the mother creates a "sexually based narcissism" (66) when male identification is blocked by the extreme devaluation of the mother, or when the mother locks her child in a fused state, blocking the formation of male identity. Asbury was locked in such a state with his mother, unable to escape—a bird locked in a cage (O'Connor 1979a).

Death of Potential: Annihilation of the Psyche
Asbury's defenses break down toward the end of "The Enduring Chill." O'Connor (1979a) wrote, "The last film of illusion [is] torn as if by a whirlwind from [Asbury's] eyes" (382) and the savage image of the bird above his bed seemed poised to attack. "He [will] live in the face of a purifying terror" (382). The dichotomy of the two words 'purifying' and 'terror' demonstrates the tension of paradox. If 'purifying' is interpreted as absolving or redeeming, it presents a religious connotation. Father Finn spoke of the power of daily prayer as a means of salvation of the soul, and yet, his words terrified Asbury. They threaten him with the "terrible pain" of "loss for all eternity" (377). The bird represented the mother. When Father Finn advised that, unless Asbury prays for the Holy Ghost to be sent to him, he will be doomed to experience loss even in death, this was more than could be contained by

the mind of Asbury. Either way, he was doomed—in life by his mother, or in death by his father.

Father Finn intended that Asbury call upon the Holy Spirit for forgiveness before he died (O'Connor 1979a). To Asbury, conjuring up the Holy Spirit would have been tantamount to conjuring up a loving father. The terms 'purifying' and 'terror', when combined, imply a kind of unholy baptism, as though the Holy Ghost is transmuted into the frightening image of the "fierce bird with spread wings" that menacingly appeared "about to descend" on Asbury's head (366). As he looked out the window at the "tree line . . . black against the crimson sky . . . it [forms] a brittle wall, standing as if it were the frail defense he had set up in his mind to protect him from what was coming" (382). Although this frightening image paralyzed the body of Asbury, his mind functioned with clarity as he entered the realm of the psychotic with "a feeble cry, a last impossible protest" (382)—like the living dead, the ultimate annihilation of the psyche. As Winnicott (1968b) explained, for the child who "has not reached unit status" of mind and body, a sense of "I AM" cannot occur (61). Therefore, life is chaotic and fragmented because there is little cohesion of the self to reckon with the external environment. The thought of death becomes a haunting experience that takes the body while leaving the vulnerable mind 'afloat'.

Summary

Asbury Fox was trapped in a symbiotically fused state with his mother (O'Connor 1979a). As a result, he was emotionally dependent upon Mrs. Fox, unable to break away. Because of his inability to separate, it became clear that he was firmly embedded in a regressed stage of absolute dependence. In this phase of infant development, there is no sense of 'I'. If Mrs. Fox was as intrusive with her son as an infant as she demonstrated with him as an adult, it could be concluded that she repeatedly impinged upon his formative ego. It appeared that Mrs. Fox was a good-enough mother initially, attending to the *physical* needs of her son. He was probably changed, fed, and treated very much like an extension of herself. It also appeared that Mrs. Fox, as narcissistic and self-absorbed as she portrayed herself to be, felt that Mr. Fox supported her when Asbury was an infant. It seemed evident, however, that Mr. Fox was unavailable much of the time with the demands of his work, which according to Mrs. Fox, included the professions of a lawyer, businessman, farmer, and politician—all achieved with an eighth-grade education.

As Asbury grew more aware, and made attempts toward separation, Mrs. Fox probably felt threatened and exerted increased dominion over him (O'Connor 1979a). Without a father to intercede, Asbury could not separate. As Winnicott (1965) purported, the Oedipal complex begins much earlier than espoused by Freud. Winnicott believed that the presence of the father is implicit from the beginning of life and incorporated into care from the mother. As the infant ego grows stronger, the father becomes an important figure in the life of the child, mediating between the mother and the infant during the separation process. The roll of the father is minimized in "The Enduring Chill" (O'Connor 1979a), as it is in the writings of Winnicott (1965), presented in "brackets or parentheses" (Phillips 1988, 6) or in the guise of priests or oral histories within the life of Asbury Fox (O'Connor 1979a). Westling (1985) stated, "There is an oedipal struggle between sons of the New South and the heroic tradition of the patriarchal family romance where the woman is revered and the father is the center of that chivalric world" (17).

Asbury lived in the shadow of his father who, in the eyes of his mother, was part of a heroic world of manners (O'Connor 1979a). Through her oral histories of Mr. Fox, Asbury inherited the declining Southern legacy of the importance of the father, which seemed to minimize the significance of Asbury. In response, Asbury denigrated the image of his father and, in doing so, he ridiculed himself. Asbury had no opportunity for repression. He was an adult dominated by, and still dependent upon, his mother. If he made any gesture toward separation, Mrs. Fox descended with the viciousness of a black-widow spider. Consequently, Asbury either denigrated or idealized the men in his life as observed in his appraisals of his biological father, Dr. Block, and Father Vogel. His perspectives of people were colored and his object relations were poor.

O'Connor (1979a) provided a glaring example of maternal impingement in her presentation of the relationship between a mother and son. Her story exemplified the psychopathology that evolves as a consequence of repeated intrusion by the mother with narcissistic needs of her own, as well as the consequences on the child with an absent father. Excessive impingement is a tragedy for any child. For Asbury, encroachment meant an "inflexible degree of narcissistic interference and an impairment in the capacity to make an internal separation" from his mother (O'Connor 1979a, 319), as well as a failure to incorporate the mind-body connection (Burgner 1985). Consequently, he remained in a symbiotically fused state, dependent upon the mother and unable to achieve his creative potential nor establish any sense of self.

The effects of inadequate mothering on Asbury (O'Connor 1979a) as an adult are striking and clearly represent an individual who remained embedded in the earliest stage of development, which Winnicott (1965) referred to as absolute dependence. Asbury exhibited a wooden and inauthentic nature, squashed creativity, dependence, and a blurring in his ability to distinguish between internal and external reality (O'Connor 1979a). He searched endlessly for that which he missed as a child—a father who would set him free and a mother who would allow him to go without retaliation.

CHAPTER 4

GOOD COUNTRY PEOPLE

Flannery O'Connor (1979b) brought the consequences of early mother-infant failure to life in her short story, "Good Country People," as she depicted the struggle for autonomy between mother and child in a rural Southern town. Again, a battling mother-child dyad is presented. However, in this particular story, O'Connor involves a daughter rather than a son in the role of the child. Unlike twenty–four-year-old Asbury Fox in "The Enduring Chill" (O'Connor 1979a), who returns home because he *thinks* he is dying, thirty–two-year-old Joy/Hulga Hopewell returns home because she is, in fact, suffering from a life-threatening heart condition. According to her doctors, "With the best of care, Joy might see forty-five" (O'Connor 1979b, 296). If it were not for this condition, "Joy had made it plain that . . . she would be far from these red hills and good country people" (276). A striking difference between Asbury and Joy/Hulga is that Asbury (O'Connor 1979a) was symbiotically fused with his mother, unable to separate, while Joy/Hulga (O'Connor 1979b) is rejected by her mother because of her looks and willfulness and is, therefore, *forced* to separate.

It is hypothesized that Joy/Hulga achieved the Winnicott (1961) second developmental stage of relative dependence, based upon her ability to create the necessary space to make use of transitional objects; namely, her artificial leg and her changed name (O'Connor 1979b). Additionally, Joy/Hulga had separated physically and emotionally from her mother; lived and thought independently; disavowed Southern tradition; and accomplished her original goals of obtaining a doctoral degree, teaching, and forging her own identity. To reach the stage of relative dependence, Joy/Hulga had to experience 'adequate' mothering during the earlier stage of absolute dependence. Although her childhood was undoubtedly not ideal, based upon her dismal personality and poor interpersonal relationships, she emanated a quality of psychic strength and willfulness in her relationship with her mother. This quality was missing in the relationship between Asbury and Mrs. Fox (O'Connor 1979a). Joy/Hulga does not experience a shared reality with her mother, but rather, a false reality that was shared with the external environment (O'Connor 1979b). One reason for the developmental difference between Joy/Hulga and Asbury may be the presence of a father in the life of Joy/Hulga until she was ten years of age (O'Connor 1979a, 1979b). Her father mediated between her and her mother, thus furthering a slightly more healthy psychological foundation (O'Connor 1979b).

Profile of a Mother

Mrs. Hopewell was Joy/Hulga's mother and a woman who generously spouted platitudes such as, "Nothing is perfect," "That is life!" and "Other people have their opinions too" (O'Connor 1979b, 273). Her use of platitudes in place of direct communication implied she was incapable of internalization or introspection. She therefore appeared more externally motivated. She was consistently affected by what the neighbors thought and desired to be regarded by them as the image of gentility stereotypically associated with 'a Southern lady'. Her name is an allegory that accurately depicts her desire to be acceptable. In reality, Mrs. Hopewell sat at the kitchen table in the morning in her red kimono with her hair done up in rags. She was a vulgar image quite unbecoming a true Southern lady who would be 'properly' attired at meals.

Mrs. Hopewell was the sole caretaker of the family farm. As such, her approach to business management seemed rather inept. She appeared to elevate the status of her hired help to near nobility because they were "good country people," even though others viewed them as "misfits" (O'Connor 1979b, 272). This was clearly apparent when their previous employer warned Mrs. Hopewell about the Freeman's, her tenant farmers. She was told that, although Mr. Freeman is a "good farmer," Mrs. Freeman was the "nosiest woman ever to walk the earth [and] she's got to be into everything" (272). Mrs. Hopewell viewed the Freeman's as a "godsend," especially since there were no other applicants for the job; she gave Mrs. Freeman "the responsibility for everything," as a means of "handling" her (272). Handling people was something Mrs. Hopewell was forced to do on her own since she divorced her husband when Joy/Hulga was ten years of age.

By making Mrs. Freeman a 'confidante', of sorts, Mrs. Hopewell created the illusion that Mrs. Freeman was not only in charge, but that she was also an equal (O'Connor 1979b). The rationale was, if Mrs. Freeman knew everything, she would be easier to handle. Mrs. Freeman involved herself in every aspect of Mrs. Hopewell's life. She stood in the kitchen, like an overseer, watching, listening, and talking as Mrs. Hopewell and her daughter sat and ate. In this manner, she elicited all the gory details surrounding the hunting accident that "literally blasted off" Joy/Hulga's leg, also at ten years of age (275). Mrs. Hopewell rationalized that she was able to "use other people's" bad qualities in a constructive way because she had "no bad qualities of her own" (272). She had a remarkable capacity to adapt reality to suit *her* needs. She reported to others that the sexually active Freeman daughters—one of whom was married and pregnant at fifteen years of age—were "two of the finest girls she knew," even though, to Easterners, these girls might be considered "white trash" (272). According to Mrs. Hopewell's thinking, although the girls were promiscuous, they captured and maintained the illusion of the 'Southern belle'—sensuous and practical. They "get their man" (273).

Profile of a Daughter
Mrs. Hopewell's own daughter, Joy/Hulga, was a "large, angry blond girl who [had] an artificial leg" (O'Connor 1979b, 271). An atheist, Joy/Hulga "lumbers" or "stumps" around the house wearing a "six-year-old skirt and a yellow sweat shirt with a faded cowboy on a horse embossed on it" (271, 276). Mrs. Hopewell viewed Joy's clothing as "idiotic" and labels her daughter as "simply . . . still a child" (276). Joy/Hulga, as any angry adolescent, made sure she did not fit in and thrived on her own eccentricity, finding her combination of clothing "funny" (276). This behavior seemed to give her a sense of power and superiority. The juxtaposition in the description of the outfit worn by Joy/Hulga creates an interesting image. It is questionable as to whether she was wearing a skirt that was six years old, or whether she was wearing the skirt of a six-year-old.

The notion of an adolescent wearing clothing that would suit a six-year-old child seems foolish, yet it was most accurate in the case of

Joy/Hulga. She displayed constantly truculent behavior that served only to accentuate the odd combination of clothing that became her consistent uniform—a skirt and sweatshirt with a "faded cowboy on it" (276). O'Connor wrote, "Mrs. Hopewell thought of her as a child [and a] poor stout girl. . . . [She would have preferred] the child had not taken the Ph.D." (271–276). Paradoxically, Winnicott (1960b) stated, "People are not their own age; they are to some extent every age or no age" (81). This was particularly true of Joy/Hulga, who was not all that clear on the question herself.

Unlike Asbury, Joy/Hulga achieved academic success after going East. She obtained a doctoral degree in philosophy and lived a seemingly autonomous life. In the East, where she was an academician, she was known as Hulga. At home, she was known only by her given name of Joy. Mrs. Hopewell refused to call her Hulga, a name Joy legally assumed at twenty-one years of age, because Mrs. Hopewell viewed it as "the ugliest name in any language" (O'Connor 1979b, 274). Just the sound of the name, and the image it evoked for her, reminded Mrs. Hopewell of the "broad blank hull of a battleship" (274). Joy selected the name Hulga because of its sound, heavy with meaning. Joy/Hulga considered her name a "personal affair," arrived at "purely on the basis of its ugly sound" (275). According to Guralnik (1980), the name Hulga is equated with the word hulk, which means "large, heavy, and often unwieldy or clumsy. Something dragged—a towed vessel; any ship; a big unwieldy ship; especially an old dismantled ship, used as a prison or the like and not intended to be seagoing; a deserted wreck or ruins; a big, clumsy person or thing" (683). Hulga was imprisoned in her own body (O'Connor 1979b). Her name gave that prison meaning. She made a virtue out of a vice. Her ugliness became her identity, also putting Mrs. Hopewell's capacity for illusion to the test.

Rejection of Maternal Conventions
The depth of antagonism felt by Joy/Hulga toward her mother and her Southern environment was reflected in her rejection of everything important to her mother including her Southern legacy and her name (O'Connor 1979b). Part of the antagonism Joy/Hulga cultivated toward her mother was due to maternal domination. Domination, in this sense, is a practice that "inhibits proper maturation" (Carlson 1996, 1). Mrs. Hopewell wanted her daughter to act 'normal' (O'Connor 1979b). She refused to accept the fact that Joy/Hulga was unattractive and deformed

because such acknowledgement would reflect back upon her in a negative fashion. Therefore, Mrs. Hopewell incorporated a form of domination, treating Joy/Hulga like a child. She attempted to inculcate acceptable, normal behavior on her daughter, hoping something might change. In so doing, Mrs. Hopewell attempted to magically transform Joy/Hulga into an idealized version of herself—a person who "had no bad qualities of her own" (272). Joy/Hulga rejected the beliefs and expectations of her mother by emotionally withdrawing into an internal world of nihilism where nothing mattered. She did this to survive in the confusing and distasteful externalized world of her mother—a world to which Joy/Hulga refused to conform.

Winnicott (1966c) described the stage before "the arrival of secondary gains when the child needs help and feels mad because of being compelled from within to steal, to destroy" (110). In this scenario, the child has a good-enough beginning, but something disrupted the process and the child's "ego defenses broke down" (110). In response, the child reorganizes its defenses, but in an inferior way, allows the "hope of compelling society to go back with him or her to the position where things went wrong, and to acknowledge this fact" (110). Winnicott further explained that, if successful, "the child can reach back to the period before the moment of deprivation and rediscover the good object and the good human controlling environment which by existing originally enabled him or her to experience impulses, including destructive ones" (110–111). Joy/Hulga went back in time to the event wherein she lost her leg and her father was still a part of her life, but she failed to engage her mother (O'Connor 1979a). Consequently, when she changed her name to Hulga she made an effort to inform the external environment of her dilemma. The environment did not acknowledge her predicament, however, so she rejected society in its entirety.

To Mrs. Hopewell, Joy/Hulga is a "large hulking [reminder of] constant outrage, [who has] obliterated every expression from her face [with] a look of someone who has achieved blindness by an act of will" (O'Connor 1979b, 273). As Winnicott (1967a) pointed out, babies who are not seen for themselves often "look around for other ways of getting something of themselves back from the environment" (112). Joy/Hulga (O'Connor 1979b) behaved like a blind infant who needed "to get [herself] reflected through other senses than that of sight" (Winnicott, 1967a, 112). However, her mother did not respond to her as if Joy/Hulga was in trouble because her mother was incapable of experiencing empathy (O'Connor 1979a). Therefore, the attempts Joy/Hulga made at communication remained frozen in her internal experience and reflected in her external appearance. According to Mrs. Hopewell, Joy/Hulga was "brilliant but doesn't have a grain of sense" (276). She seemed to view her daughter as a pathetic rebel who rejected Southern tradition for the strange values of the East. Joy/Hulga became a "poor stout girl in her thirties who had never danced a step or had any normal good times" (274). In comparison, Mrs. Hopewell viewed Mrs. Freeman's daughters as living more normal and acceptable lives—lives that Mrs. Hopewell and others could more readily understand.

Joy/Hulga intentionally set herself apart, showing flagrant disrespect and intolerance of traditional Southern ways (O'Connor 1979b). She left for college in the East and became involved in esoteric philosophical studies, which served only to widen the gap of understanding between Joy/Hulga and her mother. Conversely, Asbury Fox (O'Connor 1979a) made every attempt to fulfill the desires his mother had for him. Mrs. Hopewell equated education with separation and viewed education as the cause of the behavior displayed by Joy/Hulga (O'Connor 1979b). Her delusion was that, if Joy/Hulga had not separated from her, all would have been well. In reality, education permitted differentiation for Joy/Hulga from her mother. Mrs. Hopewell believed that philosophy ended with the Greeks and Romans and, belonging to antiquity, should remain there. The language and concepts of philosophy permitted Joy/Hulga to differentiate very thoroughly because they are logically structured, and, therefore, posed a threat to the fantasy world within which the mind of her mother resided.

Mrs. Hopewell envisioned Joy/Hulga teaching at the university as a "scarecrow lecturing to more of the same," whereas Joy/Hulga sought to be "lecturing to people who knew what she was talking about" (O'Connor 1979b, 276). Education should be a practical matter, according to Mrs. Hopewell, like becoming a schoolteacher or nurse—professions a mother could be proud of and that other people could understand. "It was nice for girls to go to school to have a good time" (276). Instead, Joy/Hulga engaged in an esoteric profession, which seems archaic and somehow dangerous to Mrs. Hopewell, with mystical writings like "some evil incantation in gibberish" (277). Mrs. Hopewell read the following excerpt from a philosophy book belonging to Joy/Hulga: "Science, on the other hand, has to assert its soberness and seriousness afresh and declare that it is concerned solely with what-is. Nothing—how can it be for science anything but a horror and a phantasm? If science is right, then one thing stands firm: science wishes to know nothing of nothing. Such is after all the strictly scientific approach to Nothing. We know it by wishing to know nothing of Nothing" (277). The words were quite analogous to the wishes of Mrs. Hopewell to know "nothing of the Nothing" that Hulga's interests and career were to her, as well as to another form of platitude that 'cuts off' thinking and feeling. Joy/Hulga arrogantly alluded to this concept when she exclaimed, "Woman! Do you ever look inside? Do you ever look inside and see what you are not?" (276). On the surface, these comments might sound insightful; however, Joy/Hulga was also limited in insight, willfully locked into a nihilistic worldview that foreclosed any hope of insight. Reason, or a balanced view of reality was lost for her in disjointed interactions with her mother. Thus, when Mrs. Hopewell shut the philosophy book, she "leaves the room as though she is having a chill" (277) because she could not understand what had become of the girl she named Joy. As Greenberg and Mitchell (1983) explained, Joy/Hulga and Mrs. Hopewell did not have a "developed language of communication" (Greenberg and Mithchell 1983, 192), which would normally be learned in an achieved mother-infant relationship. Rather, their attempts at communication were "diffuse and fragmented [as] those who manipulate concepts and who are held back by banal considerations" (Winnicott 1968b, 61).

Ironically, Joy/Hulga studied Malebranche—a philosopher crippled by spine deformity—whose emphasis was the issues of will (O'Connor 1979b). In part, his belief was that reason overcomes the negative impact of emotion. He agreed with Descartes—the father of rationalism— that awareness of mental states is immediate and infallible, whereas perception of bodies is indirect and fallible, and that knowledge of things comes from clear and distinct ideas grasped by reason and not by sensation or imagination (Fieser 1996). Mrs. Hopewell acknowledged that Joy/Hulga was intelligent; however, it was an intelligence that was something different from the common country good sense that Mrs. Hopewell valued and understood—values such as those accepted by her tenant farmers (O'Connor 1979b). Being intellectual is scary; it changes one. Mrs. Hopewell did not understand the transformation. She believed arcane intelligence was what caused Joy/Hulga to say "strange things," to become separate from other people, and increasingly transformed into something alien—"bloated, rude, and squint-eyed" (276).

Similarly, she believed that impractical book learning changes character and kept Joy/Hulga from becoming more aware of herself and more
caring of herself so "she wouldn't be so bad looking" (275). According
to Mrs. Hopewell, a more practical education would have encouraged
Joy/Hulga to have a "pleasant expression" (275). "Mrs. Hopewell said
that people who looked on the bright side of things would be beautiful
even if they were not" (275). Her words seemed to be an attempt to rectify what nature failed to accomplish. Joy/Hulga lacked beauty and
charm—intrinsic Southern values for a woman. She followed obscure
intellectual pursuits, which was frowned upon for a Southern lady.

According to Winnicott (1968b), "The intellect only knows how to
talk about wisdom" (60). If intellect is "split off," then the individual is
"split off from life" (60). In such a scenario, the individual "can function brilliantly without much reference to the human being. But it is the
human being who, by an accumulation of experiences duly assimilated,
may achieve wisdom" (60). Accordingly, Joy/Hulga (O'Connor 1979b)
is "pseudo-educated" (McFarland 1976, 16) because it is the gap between rationality and femininity that is the crux of her downfall
(O'Connor 1979b). Winnicott emphasized that the mother-infant unit
"leads to identity with wider units" (60) or, more simply, a connectedness with the environment. Relatedness is not observed between
Joy/Hulga and Mrs. Hopewell (O'Connor 1979a). Instead, Joy/Hulga
was dissatisfied at home. Accordingly, she looked outside the home for
a connection reflective of her internal state and found it in nihilistic
philosophy. The irony is that philosophical thought can be an isolated
existence; thus, philosophy became a kind of external resonance of
Joy/Hulga's internal experience.

As mentioned earlier, Mrs. Hopewell divorced her husband when
Joy/Hulga was ten years of age (O'Connor 1979b). Emotions must
have been tense and fragmented within the Hopewell home. Divorce in
the 1940s and 1950s was not only rare, but it was condemned.
Joy/Hulga may well have been afraid of also losing her mother, feeling
that her own destructive impulses may have been responsible for driving away her father. At the age of ten, Joy/Hulga lost not only her
father, but also her leg. She may also have held a childlike belief that
losing her leg was punishment for other destructive impulses.

Absence of the father creates serious difficulties within mother-
daughter relationships due to the concurrent absence of mediation.
Without a father, Joy/Hulga (O'Connor 1979b) may have experienced

an emptiness referred to as "blank mourning" (Green 1972, 146). This concept of loss is associated with object loss and/or threats of abandonment. The concurrent loss of limb experienced by Joy/Hulga within the same year could be interpreted as a form of symbolic castration. Her mother, in this instance, would be the castrator due to the divorce of her husband, cutting Joy/Hulga off from her father. Winnicott (1964b) posited,

> Every little girl has it in her to dream of being in mother's place, or at any rate of dream romantically. Mothers have to be very understanding when this sort of thing is going on. Some mothers find it much easier to stand the friendship between father and son than between father and daughter. Yet it is a great pity if the close bond between father and daughter is interfered with by feelings of jealousy and rivalry instead of being allowed to develop naturally; for sooner or later the little girl will realize the frustration that belongs to this kind of romantic attachment, and she will eventually grow up and look in other directions for the practical outcome to her imaginings. (117)

Joy/Hulga may have fantasized an association between the loss of her leg and the loss of her father because these two incidents occurred within the same year (O'Connor 1979b). Her resultant anxiety was undoubtedly extreme. She likely contained this anxiety by symbolically embodying these two losses in her wooden leg.

Creation of a Name

In addition to containing her anxiety by maintaining a connection with her father and leg via her artificial limb, Joy/Hulga also organized competing impulses of rage and fear toward her mother in the creation of her new name (O'Connor 1979b). The construction of the name Hulga both protected her mother from the full force of her destructive impulses, while maintaining a continual source of disruption. A tacit agreement not to question the origin of the name change maintained the tension between mother and daughter because Joy/Hulga did not wish to be destroyed by the anger of her mother, nor did Mrs. Hopewell have any wish to be destroyed. With the loss of her leg, Joy/Hulga learned of her mortality early in life. According to Winnicott (1967b), "When a deprivation occurs in terms of a breakup of the home, especially an estrangement between the parents, a very severe thing happens in the child's mental organization. Suddenly his aggressive ideas and impulses become unsafe. The child takes over the control that has been lost and becomes identified with the framework" (94–95).

Joy/Hulga learned that her mother, as a container, gave Joy life, but did not fill her life with joy (O'Connor 1979b). One might assume that her transition from absolute to relative dependence was tumultuous at best. Winnicott might have referred to her experience as a "relative environmental failure" (as cited in Hughes 1989, 136). However, the infant Joy/Hulga somehow discovered enough potential space to utilize her developing intellect, creatively identifying two makeshift realities—one internal and one external (O'Connor 1979b). Her intellect took over, dissociating from her body. What Joy/Hulga seemed to have lacked, however, was the conscious understanding of how these two realities, though separate, are interdependent while she unconsciously integrated both realities through the creation of her name. Consequently, her understanding of internal/external reality was distorted. Winnicott (1963b) stated, "In Absolute Dependence, if the mother has successfully devoted herself to her infant, the infant's process of development is not distorted" (86). This concept is expanded upon in the analysis of Joy's creation of the name Hulga (O'Connor 1979b). Accordingly, "the healthy individual does not become isolated, but becomes related to the environment in such a way that the individual and the environment can be said to be interdependent" (Winnicott 1963b, 84). Clearly, Joy/Hulga rejected the home environment, which she may have felt rejected her, and adopted a nihilistic worldview (O'Connor 1979b).

Joy/Hulga went East, fleeing the notion of connection with, or dependence upon, her mother (O'Connor 1979b). The emotional awareness of infant dependence upon the mother is an important stage of development within the period of relative dependence (Winnicott 1963a). Hulga did not seem to carry such awareness with her as she departed home (O'Connor 1979b). She rejected the notion of any dependence upon her mother and, therefore, any importance her mother had in her life. It is only when her body gave out that she became truly aware of her dependence. While healthy, Joy/Hulga felt no need for her mother. In fact, she consciously rejected any identification with her mother. However, the dependence emerges as Joy/Hulga created an identity for herself that was *opposite* to the identity her mother wanted for her; hence, the new identity remained related in its opposing nature.

Although the name Hulga likely reflected Joy's internal state, it also attracted external reactions from her mother and others (O'Connor 1979b). Although renaming herself Hulga was a creative act, satisfaction cannot be complete, for as Winnicott (1971b) clarified, "In a search for the self the person concerned may have produced something valuable in terms of art . . . and yet have failed to find the self that he or she is looking for. The self is not really to be found in what is made out of products of body or mind, however valuable these constructs may be in terms of . . . impact. If the artist . . . is searching for the self . . . there is already some failure . . . in the field of general creative living. *The finished creation never heals the underlying lack of sense of self*" (emphasis mine) (54–55).

Personification of an Internalized State

The name Hulga is an allusion to the mythical god, Vulcan—the ancient Roman god of fire and metalworking who is identified with the Greek Hephaestus and appears to be an amalgamation of these two gods. The name is forged to create effect, "like the ugly sweating Vulcan who stayed in the furnace" (O'Connor 1979b, 275). This image reflected the feelings of entrapment experienced by Joy/Hulga, feelings of being caught in a cauldron of emotions—a hot place that is isolated; restricted; dark; hot; smelly; and yet, powerful and potentially dangerous—a metaphorical womb. In mythology, the work of the Vulcan is energy used to create heat to, in turn, forge metal. The furnace creates heat. Heat and fire are untouchable and potentially destructive.

The Vulcan analogy is appropriate for Joy/Hulga since Vulcan, who was born lame, was so repugnant to his mother, Juno, that she flung him out of heaven (O'Connor 1979b). In the Greek version, Vulcan becomes Hephaestus who is the god of smiths and fire. He was born lame and weak and his mother Hera disliked him so intensely that she threw him down from Olympus. There is a similarity in sounds within the names Vulcan and Hulga. Vul:Hul/ can:ga becomes a vulgarization of the name Vulcan. Yet in another version, Vulcan is not a god at all, but merely a tough, practical Roman craftsman (Perowne 1969, 15).

Hulga became the antithesis of godliness or good breeding, as seen in her nihilism and rejection of manners that are important facades for Mrs. Hopewell (O'Connor 1979b). Joy/Hulga became vulgar, casting off any trace of manners as she acted in a crude and unrefined manner. Paradoxically, while acting vulgar, "instead of lacking in distinction, aesthetic value or charm," she created a distinct image designed to hurt her mother (275). Assuming Mrs. Hopewell rejected the infant Joy based upon outward appearances, as Hera rejected Vulcan/Hephaestus, the creation of Hulga tells an important story.

The name Hulga parallels creation myth, but is myopic in scope, just as Joy/Hulga is literally myopic. One might compare Joy/Hulga's act to what Grolnick (1984) referred to as an "'as if' myth which person defies the uncontrollable forces of nature (thereby weaving them into our own identity) snatched some measure of control forman in a manner similar to children making believe they are in control of projections of inner forces that cannot be directly controlled when they play at war, witches, and cops and robbers" (225). Joy/Hulga believed the formation of her new name to be "one of her major triumphs" because her mother "had not been able to turn her dust into Joy," as though she was already dead inside (O'Connor 1979b, 275). To Joy/Hulga, her "highest creative act . . . was that she had been able to turn herself into Hulga" (275). The name Hulga also parallels mechanized perfection such as an act of will—a crafted image, rather than a natural one, deliberately honed to create a reaction. The name change was also a form of "magical destruction" (Winnicott 1964b, 98). As if by magical construction, the world of Joy was annihilated by an act of will and recreated into the world of Hulga (O'Connor 1979b). This aggressive act of destroying and recreating was an attempt at organizing her world. The change became a creatively destructive act—a refusal to create the false self desired by Mrs. Hopewell.

Similar to a Vulcan tending a furnace, Hulga waited for her mother to come to her as though Joy/Hulga had the hopeless wish of an adult for a good-enough mother to enter her life (O'Connor 1979b). Instead, Joy/Hulga fantasized a more cynical version of Mrs. Hopewell as one elevated among mortals, hiding behind platitudes and Southern tradition like a misfit goddess who expected others to serve her—including Joy. After placing her mother in this light, Joy became the personification of the illusion Mrs. Hopewell needed to show to the external world. Joy punctured this illusion with her physical appearance and behavior, synthesizing both of these aspects in the name Hulga. When her mother eventually came to her, asking for help walking the land, Joy/Hulga exhibited such nastiness that her mother responded, "If you can't come pleasantly, I don't want you at all" (274). Joy/Hulga retaliated with, "If you want me, here I am—LIKE I AM" (274). She was referring, in part, to her bodily deformity.

Winnicott (1971b) explained, "What the [child] must be able to adjust to is the attitude of his mother and of other people towards his deformity and eventually it becomes necessary for [her] to see [herself] as abnormal. The normality for the child must be his own somatic shape and function. As he starts so [she] must be accepted. So [she] must be loved. It is a matter of being loved without sanctions" (263). "LIKE I AM," meaning "my body and mind as one; accept me as I am" (274). Instead, a mutual projective identification occurred between Joy/Hulga and her mother, with each imposing the most terrifying and unacceptable parts of themselves onto the other (O'Connor 1979b). Mrs. Hopewell projected ugliness and gracelessness, while Joy/Hulga projected superficiality and a hyper aura of criticism.

In her statement, "I AM," Joy/Hulga paradoxically expressed that she was both dependent and disconnected—a universal human fear of birth and growth (O'Connor 1979b, 274). She was intellectually independent and disconnected from the potential space of the South, as well as from her mother who was entrenched in Southern values. However, Joy/Hulga was also disconnected from her own psyche and physical deformity. She split her intellect between "psychosomatic existence and living" (274), literally creating in the name Hulga another false self. Through the name change, aggression was tempered by the metaphorical destruction of the mother (i.e., Joy). Yet, at the same time, the mother survived the destructive impulses via the new name of Hulga.

Winnicott (1939b) pointed out that "to be able to tolerate all that one may find in one's inner reality is one of the great human difficulties, and an important human aim is to bring into harmonious relationship one's personal inner and outer realities" (89). Joy/Hulga rejected the physical and somatic world for that of the intellectual. She rejected "dogs or cats or birds or flowers or nature or nice young men. She looked at nice young men as though she could smell their stupidity" (O'Connor 1979b, 276), implying her feelings of superiority. McFarland (1976) stated,

> Her rejection of the physical world stems from her
> awareness of its liability to imperfection. Hulga's own
> imperfection is gross—she lost a leg when she was ten—
> but O'Connor obviously intended her to be a figure of all
> mankind, which suffers from the imperfections of the
> human condition. Hulga insists on calling attention to her
> physical imperfection and refuses to try to improve her
> appearance. However, this defensive insistence that she
> be accepted "LIKE I AM" does not indicate that *she* has
> really accepted what she is; rather, it suggests that she is
> trying to insulate herself against the pain of difference
> and imperfection (emphasis mine). (37)

In this regard, the behavior demonstrated by Joy/Hulga is almost
counterphobic. For example, "I'm not ashamed; I'll rub your face in my
imperfection to prove it." However, her behavior also communicates
her ability as an infant to use her mother, as well as her consequent
ability to relate to external objects. As Winnicott (1966b) explained,

> The child needs to be able to experience the various
> kinds of object relating all in the same day or even at one
> moment; for instance, you may see a small child enjoying
> relationships with an aunt or a dog or a butterfly and the
> observer may see not only that the child is making objec-
> tive perceptions but is enjoying the enrichment that
> comes from discovery. This does not mean, however, that
> the child is ready to live in a discovered world. At any
> moment the child merges in again with a cot or the
> mother or the familiar smells and is re-established in a
> subjective environment. (1133)

Winnicott (1968b) stated, "The central feature in human development is the arrival and secure maintenance of the stage 'I AM'" (56). He
emphasized that "it implies a safe and secure journey from fusion to
separation—development toward independence—wholeness . . . even
when reaching toward independence" (56). When Hulga said, "If you
want me, here I am—LIKE I AM" (O'Connor 1979b, 274), it seemed on
the surface that she had made a safe and secure journey from fusion to
separation. It appeared that the only reason she was home was because

she was physically dependent upon her mother because she was dying. Yet her "I am" is metaphorically in the lower case. It is the 'empty hull of a battleship that is badly listing'. However, Joy/Hulga exists. It is her 'hull.' She has been attacked, yet she continues to endure.

The relationship between Joy/Hulga and her mother defied closeness (O'Connor 1979b). In fact, it appeared that Mrs. Hopewell was not at all in tune with the needs of her child, and vice versa. It could also be assumed that Mrs. Hopewell had never been completely empathic with the needs of her daughter and, instead, imposed her own needs upon the infant Joy. For Joy/Hulga, there was a sense of authenticity in being Joy because naming her infant Joy was her mother's attempt to compensate herself through her infant. It seemed that Joy/Hulga and her mother engaged in 'splitting'—the mother's fluffy 'Joy' with the daughter's heavy, ugly Hulga. Splitting is not only a defense used by mother and daughter, but for Joy/Hulga, it was a way of organizing her experiences. According to Ogden (1986), "Splitting is a boundary creating mode of thought and therefore a part of an order-generating (not yet a personal meaning-generating) process" (48).

The name Joy ends with an inflection—Joi-ee—that is optimistic in sound. When pronounced, the utterance of the name leaves a perceptible smile on the face of the speaker because the muscles near the chin and cheek are impressed into service. Joy is lightness/happiness similar to the platitudes uttered by Mrs. Hopewell. Yet, the name does not reflect the individual. The name Joy is, in essence, the mother's false self. It is an imposed veneer, painted for external acceptance. Joy is what Mrs. Hopewell wanted to present to the world, but was not the feeling she had for her child (O'Connor 1979b). The name Hulga, on the other hand, has no inflection. It is a flat, harsh two-syllable sound. When pronounced, one's lips do not move. The tongue produces the sound; the lips are not involved. Thus, the name can be pronounced flatly with no movement of the face.

Renaming herself Hulga was an aggressive and destructive act by Joy directed toward her mother (O'Connor 1979b). She unconsciously attempted to show the world the injustice done to her and consciously attempted to 'turn the tables' on her mother by demonstrating her own displeasure and rejection. Unfortunately, her defenses were crudely forged, based upon the probability of poor early environmental beginnings; yet, those defenses were also somewhat effective. She defeated her mother daily, but could not change her. She sought some kind of satisfaction in her mother's reactions. In this way, she magically destroyed the illusion of joy that Mrs. Hopewell presented to the world, and instead, portrayed a very different image.

The pent-up aggressive energy that emerged in Joy/Hulga was paradoxical in nature (O'Connor 1979b). What was designed to antagonize her mother and gain her attention became a self-destructive act. This was evidenced when Mrs. Freeman saw through the guise of Joy and addressed her as Hulga. Mrs. Freeman, as her allegorical name implies, was free enough from the situation to clearly see what was actually taking place. She was ruled by cynicism and had the perspective to look beyond facades. She observed the self-created distortion of Joy/Hulga, which had the ultimate potential for destruction (Fitzgerald 1975). The observations of Mrs. Freeman were penetrating. Her "beady steel-pointed eyes had penetrated far enough behind her face to reach some secret fact" (O'Connor 1979b, 275). She saw behind the hulking and crudely constructed name not only an emotionally broken heart, yearning to be mended by the mother, but also a physically deformed body that sought acceptance by the mother.

In part, Joy/Hulga would have liked to have destroyed her mother, but she could not, for along with all the destructive impulses, she also had love for her mother (O'Connor 1979b). Therefore, she turned the full force of her destructive potential upon herself by changing her name, thereby symbolically turning herself inside out. By this act, she vicariously hurt her mother, but in a less destructive manner. Winnicott (1939b) stated that the infant "hurts those of whom he is very fond" (86). Naming herself Hulga was a way of making the inner relation tolerable—a dramatization of a "too-awful inner world" (90). He added, "When the cruel and destructive forces [of inner reality] threaten to dominate over the loving, the individual has to do something to save himself, and one thing he does is to turn himself inside out, to dramatize the inner world outside, to act the destructive role himself and to bring about control by external authority" (89). Joy/Hulga clearly performed this act through her name change, her looks, and her actions (O'Connor 1979b).

The aggressiveness the infant Joy experienced may have overwhelmed her because there was no outlet for the residual feelings (O'Connor 1979b). Infants naturally seem to enjoy flailing their limbs and crying lustily while venting aggressive impulses. Joy/Hulga may not have learned that aggressive drives can be quieted when combined with a sense of gratification. For example, becoming excited by the breast, hungrily wanting to devour its contents, or even to destroy it, and being given the space to have these impulses without destroying the mother while concurrently suckling until sated. Instead, Joy/Hulga might have been rebuffed for biting, thereby learning that aggressive impulses are not acceptable. In a healthy situation, when these impulses are combined with loving ones, the infant experiences satisfaction. Thus, the infant can have the initial destructive feelings, subsequently finding relief for the aggressive feelings through crying, physical movement, biting, and/or suckling. Upon satisfaction, the infant feels at peace. However, when destructive impulses cannot be expressed while being fused with loving ones, the infant is overwhelmed. Joy/Hulga may well have been quite frustrated as an infant.

Transitional Objects

Name

The name Hulga is parallel to the impenetrable suit of armor created by Vulcan (Holme 1979). In a defensive maneuver, Joy/Hulga attempts to create an impervious facade through her created name (O'Connor 1979b). The name becomes a transitional object, a connection between 'me' and 'not me', both related to, and separate from, the experience of her mother. If it is assumed that the feelings portrayed by Mrs. Hopewell toward her infant Joy were mirrored on her face, contradicting her pleasant words, then Joy/Hulga achieved an identity through this projection, maintaining a lost true self in the midst of irrationality. To do this, Joy/Hulga needed to destroy certain facets of herself before recreating them to match her own internal state. Only then could she feel real. This is her creative act through an act of will. The name became a dialectic between creativity and heritage, separateness and union.

The ability of Joy/Hulga (O'Connor 1979b) to make the name change—an action—and to tolerate the paradox of pseudoknowledge, indicated that she had the ability for a type of creative play, even though not fully realized. However, as Winnicott (1971b) maintained, "The finished creation never heals the underlying lack of self" (55). He added, "One has to allow for the possibility that there cannot be a complete destruction of a human individual's capacity for creative living and that, even in the most extreme case of compliance and the establishment of a false personality, hidden away somewhere there exists a secret life that is satisfactory because of its being creative or original to that human being. Its unsatisfactoriness must be measured in terms of its being hidden, its lack of enrichment through living experience" (86).

Vulcan is a male image, which is both potent and inspires thoughts of power (Holme 1979). Joy/Hulga may have found her father to be a mighty influence (O'Connor 1979b). At age ten, a young girl was impressed with her father's strength, often looking upon him in heroic terms. She looked to him for protection and increased personal strength. Although lame, Vulcan is a male with the ability to throw thunderbolts (Holme 1979). He possesses a penis and attributes that translate into power. The only power Joy/Hulga could muster was the elicited shock value when her mother reacted to the use of her name Hulga (O'Connor 1979b). The identity confusion evident in Joy/Hulga is analogous to the amalgamation of the facets and versions of Vulcan as a god, or merely a tough, practical, nonintellectual man who toils in the furnace room—versions Joy/Hulga attempted to paste together into a cohesive whole. Within this admixture of demigods and practical men, Joy/Hulga, through the name Hulga, tried to forge a link between her and her lost father.

According to Winnicott (1964b), if a girl loves her father, "but mother belittles all men and spoils the whole show," the child utilizes a rich fantasy life "and [her] feelings are violent" (185). It follows then that, if Mrs. Hopewell was unhappy with her husband, this attitude would have been passed on to her daughter (O'Connor 1979b). The subsequent image held by Joy/Hulga of her father would be distorted and confusing. However, "fathers can compensate for the relative failures" of maternal care (Winnicott 1957, 37). Consequently, the desire demonstrated by Joy/Hulga (O'Connor 1979b) to connect with her father through the heroic image, generated via creation of her new name, was a desire to rectify the maternal failure (Winnicott 1957).

Father. It is a young Bible salesman, not her father, who intervened, educating Joy/Hulga on her true uniqueness through his odd interest in her artificial leg (O'Connor 1979b). Joy/Hulga, by an act of will, believed in nothing and no one until this young salesman seduced her and 'called her bluff'. Manley Pointer, who was not yet a man, but pointing in that direction, was from Willohobie. He was "a tall gaunt hatless youth" of nineteen, wearing "a bright blue suit and yellow socks that were not pulled up far enough" (277). Manley presented himself at the Hopewell farm under the guise of selling Bibles. What he was really fascinated with was the wooden leg belonging to Joy/Hulga. Even though he was a 'hayseed,' Manley possessed a degree of power solely due to his maleness. An artist at seduction, he smothered Joy/Hulga with 'sweet talk' to gain access to her limb.

Through a reverent act of foreplay, in which he paid idolatrous attention to her artificial leg, Manley brought Joy into Hulga, replacing emptiness with possibility (O'Connor 1979b). To Manley, the false leg was equivalent to a religious icon as it solemnly joined the other bizarre objects in his valise. The objects seem to represent noble manifestations of Manley's desire to patch together his own deficient identity through the collection of perverse, yet revered, objects. He talked himself into the Hopewell parlor by saying to Mrs. Hopewell, "Lady, I've come to speak of serious things" (278). He informed that he came not so much from a *place,* but "just from near a place" known as Willohobie, and that he devoted himself to "Christian service" (279). He carried a heavy valise allegedly containing Bibles, which he claimed to sell to lost souls. He quoted, "He who loses his life shall find it" (280). This biblical echo heralded the later epiphany experienced by Joy/Hulga.

Initially, Mrs. Hopewell did not like Manley Pointer. He was intrusive, he took her for a fool, and his presence made her uncomfortable by reminding her of the difference in their class status. As Manley glanced around the parlor, she thought, "He has never been in a room as elegant as this" (O'Connor 1979b, 278). She was ashamed that she did not have a Bible in the parlor; however, her daughter was an atheist and forbid her to do so. Mrs. Hopewell lied and advised Manley that their Bible was on the bed stand when it was actually hidden away in the attic. Manley used guilt to win Mrs. Hopewell over. "'I'm just a country boy," he says, glancing up into her unfriendly face. "People like you don't like to fool with country people like me" (278). With this, Mrs. Hopewell cried, "Why! . . . Good country people are the salt of the earth!" (279). After Manley informed her that, in lieu of college, his desire was to devote his life to "Christian service," Mrs. Hopewell invited him to dinner, despite the protestations of Joy/Hulga (279). Manley also revealed his life-threatening heart condition by saying, "When you know it's something wrong with you and you may not live long, well then, lady" (279). Manley assureed himself a place at the dinner table with those words, even though Mrs. Hopewell regretted inviting him the moment the words left her mouth.

Mrs. Hopewell saw a connection between Joy/Hulga and Manley— both are dying and both are social outcasts (O'Connor 1979b). Dinner was strained. Joy/Hulga either ignored Manley or cast sidelong glances at him while Mrs. Hopewell felt pressured to 'take up the slack' in the conversation. She was embarrassed by the "deliberate rudeness" of Joy/Hulga (280), even though she had "lived with it, and she felt she had always to overflow with hospitality to make up for Joy's lack of courtesy" (280). Although Mrs. Hopewell found Manley boring and unsophisticated, her Southern manners precluded her from dismissing him. Consequently, when dinner was over, Joy/Hulga "cleared the dishes off the table and disappeared" (280). Mrs. Hopewell sat with Manley for two hours, fighting yawns as she listened to him talk until she made up an excuse to get him to leave. Lingering at the door after his departure, Mrs. Hopewell observed Joy/Hulga in the distance, standing in the road, as Manley approached her. Mrs. Hopewell watched Joy/Hulga and Manley talking and then walking toward the gate together.

That night, Joy/Hulga fantasized about the conversation she and Manley would have the following morning when she met him at the gate—a conversation filled with "profound implications" (O'Connor 1979, 283). She envisioned seducing Manley in the barn. Her imagined methods of seduction seem innocent and childlike, those of someone "who has not been kissed before" (285). Montgomery (1981) posited that Joy/Hulga was not an innocent. Rather, he believed her state was one of "willful ignorance" (439). While it is true that she was willful and headstrong, Joy/Hulga also exhibited a true innocence with regard to interpersonal relationships (O'Connor 1979b). She had never kissed nor engaged in any physical relationships. This was evident in her interplay with Manley.

According to Winnicott (1968b), "Object-relating can be described in terms of the experience of the subject" (227). Joy/Hulga experienced her artificial limb as a private affair—something she did not share with anyone (O'Connor 1979b). Therefore, she was confused as to how to react when Manley fervently attempted to touch her leg, much less when he asked to see where it was attached to her body. His request was an extremely intimate gesture to Joy/Hulga. She used the leg to walk—as a means of independence—however, she related to the object on a more ethereal plane, as though it was a facet of her soul. Joy/Hulga viewed Manley as shallow, with foolish religious notions. She overtly pictured her imagined seduction as a diversion from her dreary life—a kind of amusing deception from which she could even receive a degree of gratification. However, this type of defensive thinking seemed closer to rationalization than a willful act. The rationalization served as a suit of armor, protecting her emotional state while separating her from the act of living. It is rather comical to imagine Joy/Hulga capable of seducing anyone.

The seduction game began the previous day when they met near the gate after dinner, when Joy/Hulga told Manley she was seventeen. She told Manley this lie after he gazed at her with "open curiosity and fascination, like a child watching a new fantastic animal at the zoo" (O'Connor 1979b, 283). A childlike dialogue ensued between them. He looked at her "with a gaze of complete admiration" as he stated with no hesitation, and quite directly, that she had a wooden leg, while Joy/Hulga stood "blank and solid and silent" (283). Manley asked her name and she replied with Hulga. He said he had never heard of "anybody name Hulga before" as he and pointed to her shyness (284). Manley disarmed Joy/Hulga with his apparent innocence and bold words.

Manley and Joy/Hulga met the following morning, which eventually led to the hayloft (O'Connor 1979b). Here, Joy/Hulga experienced her first kiss, which was wet and noisy. Manley proceeded to not only plead for words of love, but to also ask for a specific act of love. He requested that Joy/Hulga show him where her wooden leg joined her body. The importance of this object to Joy/Hulga was magnified: "No one ever touched it but her" (288).

Connection to Father and the External World

At first, Joy/Hulga refused to show Manley where the wooden leg connected to her body. She simply told him that it connected to her knee. She was concerned that Manley would be more fascinated with the object than with her. Manley stated, "It's the thing that makes you different.

You ain't like anybody else" (O'Connor 1979b, 288). Joy/Hulga noted the wisdom in those words, as she stared into what she believed to be the eyes of innocence. However, her view was without perfect vision for Manley deftly removed the glasses from her face, slipping them into his pocket. Hulga impulsively surrendered to Manley's request, which felt "like losing her own life and finding it again, miraculously, in his" (289). She allowed Manley to see the artificial limb "in a white sock and brown flat shoe . . . bound in a heavy material like canvas . . . ending in an ugly jointure where it attached to the stump" (289). Reverently, Manley asked to be shown how to take it on and off as he handled the wooden leg "as tenderly as if it were a real one" (289). He removed the leg out of Hulga's reach. She imagined running away with Manley and allowing him the intimacy of putting the leg on and off each day. When she asked Manley to return the leg, he assured her that she had *him,* and that he would return it momentarily.

Joy/Hulga felt frightened, for "without the leg she felt entirely dependent on him" (O'Connor 1979b, 289). In this moment, the extent of the vulnerability consuming her was evident. In addition to its purpose toward mobility, the leg was also a "symbol of social bonding [allowing] individuals to approach one another [as it] promotes contact and removes separation and therefore derives its importance from the social order. . . . The leg is to the body of society what the penis is to the human body" (Chevalier and Gheerbrant 1996, 594). In light of this statement, it could be said that Joy/Hulga was castrated as a result of the hunting accident twenty years earlier when her leg was shot off (O'Connor 1979b). In its place, the wooden leg became a kind of penile appendage allowing her to function, albeit in a rather grotesque and mechanical manner. The leg, in this light, was pertinent to her interaction with Manley.

The artificial limb represented a connection to two important events in the life of Joy/Hulga—the departure of her father and the loss of her limb (O'Connor 1979b). Both events coincided in her tenth year. She imbued the object of her artificial leg with great care and reverence as though it was a wooden marker memorializing two great tragedies. The limb was connected to her father, but not to society or her mother. It served as a source of power, like a prosthetic phallus welding together some kind of cohesion. The leg also became a transitional object, but not one created as a representation of her mother. Rather, it assumes a paternal significance. Consequently, when Manley treated her leg with great admiration, he demonstrated a form of paternal tenderness. In that moment, Joy/Hulga was so taken with Manley's understanding of the importance of her leg (i.e., "She took care of it as someone else would his soul" [288]), that she was willing to give herself over to him. Through the eyes and actions of Manley, Joy/Hulga learned she was special. "You ain't like anybody else," Manley had said (288). However, Joy/Hulga later learned that what she thought was real was not. The acts and words from Manley were lies, and his interest merely in the object that provided him perverse pleasure and helped to piece together his own deficient identity.

After taking the leg from Joy/Hulga, Manley refused to return it. Instead, he removed a series of items from his valise and placed them before her, "like one presenting offerings at the shrine of a goddess" (O'Connor 1979b, 289). One item is a hollow Bible with a whiskey flask inside; another is a deck of cards with obscene pictures on them; and the other a condom with the words, "THIS PRODUCT TO BE USED ONLY FOR THE PREVENTION OF DISEASE" on the box (289). Shocked, Hulga attempted to reason with Manley by appealing to his good country stock and religious notions. She then discovered that, like her, he did not "believe in that crap!" and he went on to say, "I may sell Bibles but I know which end is up and I wasn't born yesterday and I know where I'm going" (290). With this string of clichés, Manley swept up the wooden limb that "distinguished Hulga from other people" and jammed it into his suitcase.

Hulga later learned that Manley, this collector of oddities, had also seduced a glass eye from another woman using his innocent techniques of romanticism. In such a scenario, the artificial leg and the glass eye take on a carnal quality (O'Connor 1979b). Both objects simulate parts of the human body. These particular body parts are unconsciously associated with sexual organs, the leg representing an erect penis and the eye standing for an organ containing "erectile tissue and so is capable of changing when excited" (Winnicott 1948, 87). Hence, the perversity of Manley is magnified when Joy/Hulga observed how her leg added meaning to his growing collection of perpetually aroused erotic objects (O'Connor 1979b).

The parting words offered by Manley were demeaning, equating the rejection of religion voiced by Joy/Hulga with her acquisition of education. Manley implied that he, in contrast, was an original thinker when he said, "You ain't so smart. I been believing in nothing ever since I was born!" (O'Connor 1979b, 291). This disclosure cunningly revealed a natural-born cynicism, which in contrast, made the willful and practiced nihilistic viewpoint held by Joy/Hulga seem grotesque. With her artificial leg arranged between two Bibles—one of which was the hollow whiskey concealer—Manley descended the hayloft ladder. Hulga sat in the dim light of the hayloft, watching through an opening as Manley successfully escaped across the pasture.

Deformity

The description of the artificial limb belonging to Joy/Hulga was stark and grotesque (O'Connor 1979b). The leg was a composition of rough and heavy materials, twisted and forged into a colorless form that attached to her remaining stump. As mentioned earlier, the limb was a very private object for Joy/Hulga with complicated meaning. "As a child she had sometimes been subject to feelings of shame but education had removed the last traces of that as a good surgeon scrapes for cancer" (288). On the other hand, "she took care of it as someone else would his soul, in private and almost with her own eyes turned away," like a phallic woman (288).

Over time, as Winnicott (1971b) documented, "the child has to recognize the fact of the deformity. . . . What the [child] must be able to adjust to is the attitude of his mother and others toward his deformity, and eventually it becomes necessary for him to see himself as abnormal. . . . At the start, however, the normality for the child must be his own somatic shape and function. As he starts so he must be accepted. So he must be loved. It is a matter of being loved without sanctions" (263–264). Deformity has a negative connotation, similar to the "dark beings" in folklore who are equated with the power of darkness and special powers (Chevalier and Gheerbrant 1996, 282). In this regard, "all deformities are signs of mysteries which may be either benign or malign. Like all anomalies, the first emotion they arouse may be one of repugnance, but this is a ground or a sign of being favored, by the concealment of something very precious which requires great pains if it is to be acquired. This explains the mingled fear and respect in which African society holds the feeble-minded, the halt and, especially, the blind, the latter being judged able to see beyond the outward appearance of things" (282).

Joy/Hulga did not begin her life with a deformity from birth; although, Mrs. Hopewell implied that the appearance of her daughter left something to be desired (O'Connor 1979b). Being ugly would have been bad enough for the young Joy/Hulga, but to have also had a leg 'blasted off' at the age of ten must have been devastating. The magnitude of value Mrs. Hopewell placed upon outward appearance, coupled with her inability to provide emotional support, would have most certainly created a recipe for internal disaster for Joy/Hulga who may also have endured serving as the object of curiosity throughout her hometown. Deformity "makes its victim the benign or malign intercessor between the known and the unknown, the dark and the bright side of nature, this world and the beyond" (Chevalier and Gheerbrant 1996, 282). Deformity shaped the identity of Joy/Hulga (Mitchell 1995).

When Manley took perverse pleasure in the limb he ultimately absconded from Joy/Hulga, "handling it as tenderly as if it were a real one," a sexual quality emerges (O'Connor 1979b, 289). According to Chevalier and Gheerbrant (1996), "Some deformities or infirmities, such as club-foot or the complete or partial paralysis of a limb, are charged with strong erogenous powers" (282). As Manley seduced Hulga, the leg, in turn, seduced Manley (O'Connor 1979b) like a child who wished to "get to wholeness through another that cannot be achieved in the self" (Winnicott 1968b, 61). As a result, a dormant desire was awakened in Joy/Hulga. "She felt as though her heart had stopped and left her mind to pump her blood"(O'Connor 1979b, 289). Her eyes gazed upon what she perceived to be 'real innocence'. This boy, "with an instinct that came from beyond wisdom, had touched the truth about her" (289). From the passion fueled by knowledge, her "round freezing-blue eyes" began to melt (289). For the first time since childhood, Joy/Hulga experienced passion. As she sat "face to face" with Manley, succumbing to his request to remove her limb, she experienced a vulnerability and freedom that was "like losing her own life and finding it again, miraculously, in his" (289). This refrain echoes the biblical words quoted by Manley: "He who loses his life shall find it" (280)—an incomplete echo of the redemptive words of Christ taken out of context: "He that findeth his life shall lose it: and he that loseth his life for my sake shall find it" (Matt. 10:39 KJV). This biblical allusion equated Joy/Hulga to a lost soul who found enlightenment from another. The 'other' in this situation is Manley, a perverted savior who is equated to Christ. This further exemplifies the Winnicott concept of paradox in that the individual can only achieve a *sense* of wholeness from another.

Epiphany

Epiphany, used in the current context, is a term appropriated by James Joyce from the religious sense and adapted to a more terrestrial context to the common man by Shloss (1980), as is evident in the following excerpt: "Joyce emphasizes the role of man's mind and imagination. What is revealed is not divinity in the classic sense of an independent deity, but a timeless brilliance previously unperceived; or it is the self that is seen with harsh honesty" (106). The experience of Joy/Hulga (O'Connor 1979b) was much like a vulgarized version of the fairytale *Sleeping Beauty*. Passion was asleep in her for twenty-two years. She insulated herself from the world and hid her feelings behind the guise of intellectualism. Manley, a perverse 'country bumpkin' version of Prince Charming, found her and kissed her cheek, "making little noises like a fish," thus awakening the dormant passion within her (287). Once awakened, Joy/Hulga was able to see a world filled with hope as she imagined she and Manley running off together and "every night he would take the leg off and every morning put it back on again" (289). Joy/Hulga imagined that, together, they would share a kind of intimacy she had never experienced with another person.

The fantasy indulged by Joy/Hulga was cut short when she learned that Manley collected unusual 'objects d'art.' What she actually learned from observing and listening to Manley was that what she actually received was a 'cold dose' of reality. She gazed into his "eyes [which are] like two steel spikes" (O'Connor 1979b, 289) only to discover that Manley was not the 'good ol' boy' she originally believed him to be and that he had, in essence, 'duped' her. Malebranche held that the will is determined toward the good, and that God is the most perfect being and the most perfect goodness (as cited in "Nicholas Malebranche [1638–1715]," 1999). It is an imperfection, indeed, the essence of sin, to love a less perfect being to a greater extent than a perfect being (Fieser 1996). Manley professed his love for Joy/Hulga, who was less than perfect (O'Connor 1979b). Therefore, according to Malebranche, his will was not determined toward the good because he loved an imperfect being. The recognition of this harsh reality forced Joy/Hulga to recognize just how 'out of touch' with reality she had been.

Joy/Hulga learned from Manley that two things are true—(a) she is unique, and (b) her artificial leg did indeed set her apart (O'Connor 1979b). However, she also discovered from the short encounter with Manley the true meaning of being dependent in the world. To experience passion with another being was parallel to dying and being reborn. Hulga lost her artificial limb; however, she gained a "sudden illumination" (Shloss 1980, 106). Manley foretold the fate of Joy/Hulga at his initial meeting at the Hopewell home. He quoted, "He who loses his life shall find it," but insight does not come easily (O'Connor 1979b, 280). As Manley broadened her vision, he also took something from her. Consequently, for Joy/Hulga, epiphany came with loss—not only of her leg, but of previously held beliefs. After her world was turned upside down, she used these beliefs against herself (McFarland 1976). She learned that the "lowest and ugliest and most grotesque creatures are no less capable than the intelligent and well-informed that transcendence is to be found not through escaping from the limitations of the body but, paradoxically, through embracing physical realities that the human mind finds repellant" (26). Such destruction becomes the "unconscious backcloth for love of a real object" (Winnicott 1968b, 227). Therefore, when Manley took the artificial leg belonging to Joy/Hulga, he not only unwittingly destroyed her illusion of omnipotence, but he replaced that illusion with the reality of her limitations (O'Connor 1979b). Through destruction of her illusion, Manley provided Joy/Hulga the opportunity to see that she could survive despite loss. In this regard, she received from Manley a "shared reality," which she could use and "which can feed back other-than-me substance" into her awareness (Winnicott 1968b, 227).

Summary

Joy/Hulga was an ugly, dying, crippled nihilist thirty-two years of age. Her mother was ashamed of her education, her appearance, her artificial leg, and her name change. Winnicott (1970) posited that the "main experiences [of a child] may be re-enacted by the child in his or her own home during adolescence. If the first had had reality, the second is more likely to have reality too" (285). Joy/Hulga, who was forced to return home because of illness, behaved like an angry adolescent (O'Connor 1979b). She stomped around the house on a wooden leg, exhibited a dour face, and wore an odd combination of clothing. At home, she faced her mother and Southern culture—the very things she fled on her journey East—plus the two important losses in her life of her father and her leg. Her leg was replaced by a wooden limb, but her father cannot be substituted. She stood out within the community as fatherless and deformed.

According to Winnicott (1964b), "Only when the strict and strong father figure is in evidence can the child regain his primitive love impulses, his sense of guilt, and his wish to mend" (116). Joy/Hulga could not communicate with her mother due to the absence of a common language (O'Connor 1979b). She hid her true self behind intellectualization and a name to maintain separation from her mother. Observation of the interaction between Mrs. Hopewell and Joy/Hulga indicated a great deal of aggressive impulses passing between them that seemed out of control. Although Joy/Hulga accomplished an education, she was not successful at interpersonal relationships. There was no father to mediate between Mrs. Hopewell and her daughter to help create stability in the home or to provide a role model of male-female interaction.

Mrs. Hopewell divorced her husband when Joy/Hulga was ten years of age (O'Connor 1979b). Mrs. Hopewell hints of his infidelity when she speaks of the "white trash" wives of the tenant farmers—"not the kind you would want to be around you for very long" (273–274). How Joy/Hulga lost her leg is another mystery. She focused her destructive urges on a name she derived from the powerful Vulcan. Vulcan may represent the idealized lost father. Thus, by creating her name, she preserved her father (Sterba 1940). In her relationship with Manley, Joy/Hulga had an opportunity for creative activity, imaginative playing through thoughts of seduction, and constructive work (O'Connor 1979b). These experiences allowed her to psychically and viscerally experience her destructiveness through her primitive, impulsive, and brief loving experiences with Manley. Thus, when Hulga sat in the hayloft staring out at Manley running away through the field, she not only lost something concrete, but she gained insight through an internal connection. Joy/Hulga discovered that her body, although disconnected from her wooden leg, indeed remained connected with her psyche.

It could be deduced that Joy/Hulga had achieved the Winnicott (1957) developmental stage of relative dependence, based upon her ability to create and utilize transitional objects (O'Connor 1979b). For creativity to emerge, however, Joy/Hulga had to have received good-enough environmental provisions during the first stage of absolute dependence (O'Connor 1979b; Winnicott 1957). Although her childhood may not have been ideal, there was a different quality about the relationship Joy/Hulga had with her mother than that experienced by Asbury Fox with his mother, which was likely linked to the influence of her father as a mediating factor (O'Connor 1979a, 1979b). Joy/Hulga (O'Connor 1979b) was able to separate from her mother and actually leave home to go to school. She possessed a sense of self, even though it was somewhat destructive. She relinquished her birth name; adopted nihilism; and, by an act of will, redefined herself. She stood up to her mother and replaced Joy with Hulga. Her naivete became a transitional representation of her internal state, as well as a means of separation from both Mrs. Hopewell and her mother's illusion of Joy. The artificial leg is another object imbued with special meaning for Joy/Hulga. She was able to make a connection with another person (i.e., Manley) via her leg. The ability to utilize an object (i.e., her artificial leg), which was separate while a part of herself, as a means of communication with Manley, is an advanced concept. The fantasies associated with this relationship are immature; however, the idea of a shared communication indicated the capability of object relations that Asbury (O'Connor 1979a) was unable to attain.

CHAPTER 5

CONCLUSION

This study investigated the importance of the mother on the psychic growth of infants, as well as the role of the absent father on the mother-child dyad. The mother/adult-child relationships in the two Flannery O'Connor (1979a, 1979b) short stories were examined through the 'lens' of D. W. Winnicott (1966a, 1966b, 1966c, 1966d) and his developmental model. Based upon the interaction of these two parent-child dyads, the behavior of Asbury Fox appropriately demonstrated difficulties Winnicott associated with the primary phase of absolute dependence, while Joy/Hulga Hopewell had advanced, albeit clumsily, to the next phase of the toddler—relative dependence (Oconnor 1979a, 1979b; Winnicott, 1957). These case studies demonstrated universal themes brought by today's patients to the therapeutic setting.

Winnicott (1966a, 1966b, 1966c, 1966d) posited that the human psyche has not only a will to survive, but that it is also 'hardwired' to do so. Applying a Darwinian template, he believed that the infant psyche evolves in stages. He maintained that the newborn requires complete adaptation by the environment to his needs during the period of absolute dependence. An equivalent is the mother bird that sits on her eggs, keeping them at the required temperature until the appropriate time for hatching. With the newborn infant, the psyche has not yet been born. He can be compared to the baby bird prior to hatching, encased in a hard shell and protected by a thin membrane that requires homeostasis until it is ready to emerge. Hatching of the infant nascent psyche begins with the awareness of, and progressive adaptation to, the environment. Winnicott (1966a, 1966b, 1966c, 1966d) addressed the need for gradual withdrawal by the mother from the initial emotional enmeshment with her infant as a means of guiding the infant from ego fusion toward separation and development of self. Winnicott (1964a) stated, "By taking each infant through this vital stage in early develop- ment in a sensitive way the mother gives time for her infant to acquire all sorts of ways of dealing with the shock of recognizing the existence of a world that is outside his or her magical control" (221). As the baby bird tenaciously fights to emerge from its shell, the psyche of the healthy human infant travels the hazardous journey from absolute de- pendence and relative dependence to ultimately arrive at the stage known as toward independence—a sequence referred to by Winnicott as going-on-being.

There is a kindness and optimism in the philosophy of Winnicott (1964b) that is clearly evident within his publications. He maintained that the potential for change is always within each individual, merely 'waiting' to be cultivated. He believed that a child who is unsuccessful in navigating an earlier stage of development is not doomed for failure. Rather, he felt that psychological development was always possible. He trained analysts to understand the importance of the holding environ- ment in the analytic setting, as well as the role of the good-enough mother/analyst in facilitating space for psychic growth. According to Winnicott (1960b), "Dependent or deeply regressed patients can teach the analyst more about early infancy than can be learned from direct observation of infants" (141). Through transference, the analyst can 'piece together' missing historical gaps in the lives of patients who show their expectations and needs during dependent phases.

Literature Versus Case Studies
The selected literature chosen over actual case studies offered the most distorted examples of mother-infant disruptions, useful as teach- ing tools exemplifying the Winnicott (1970) theory. The short stories authored by O'Connor (1979a, 1979b) were the focus of this study be- cause this writer exposed the rawness and darkness in all of us through her mother/adult-child dyads (as cited in Eigen 1985). They are stun- ning examples of early developmental problems that can inhibit the process of individuation. Eigen described the destruction in the O'Connor characters expressing "a baby's wrath aimed at flaws in those others. They stay caught on one horn of the process; no proper holding response allows the transition from wrath to love" (339). In "The Enduring Chill" and "Good Country People," both Asbury Fox (O'Connor 1979a) and Joy/Hulga Hopewell (O'Connor 1979b) are "hungry for identity" (Eigen 1985, 342).

Holland (1993) documented an interesting observation of psychoanalysis and literature. He maintained that psychoanalysis deals with the minds of people, whereas literature deals with their words. He added, "There is no way one can apply psychoanalysis to literature directly. Therefore we have to make some kind of bridge between the person Psychoanalysis [*sic*] talks about the words the literary critic talks about" (9). Holland posited that literature is read in an attempt to understand the viewpoint of the author; however, the pastor/counselor seeks to understand the viewpoint surrounding the literary example. While literature itself holds value, it is the human reaction to literature that most interests the pastor/counselor. Holland added that all people bring spiritual and moral judgements to their interpretations of literature. "Readers make moral judgements about life based on their own religious and spiritual agendas as they read. What we might quickly dismiss as simple opinions are actually insights into the readers psychological and spiritual inner world. This occurs whether the reader is reading sacred scripture or the Sunday comics. We reveal who we are through our identification with or rejection of the characters in the story" (12–13).

Infants define themselves through the mirrored reflection of the faces of their mothers. Winnicott (1960b) explained that the ego of the mother is fused with that of her infant during the stage of absolute dependence. He described the experience in the following manner: "The first mirror is the mother's face and . . . one of the functions of the mother . . . is to provide a mirror, figuratively speaking, in which the child can see himself or herself" (497). The mirror role of the mother is a preverbal manifestation of communication. In a healthy situation, the mother gives herself over completely to her infant, looking with intense love at her baby. In unhealthy mother-infant interactions, the mother "reflects her own mood" (Winnicott 1971b, 112). Winnicott further stated, "Many babies . . . do have to have a long experience of not getting back what they are giving. . . . They look and they do not see themselves. . . . As a result they're own creative capacity begins to atrophy, and in some way or other they look around for other ways of getting something of themselves back from the environment" (112).

Eigen (1985) described the nonparanoid healthy aspects of the visual experience of infants. He stated, "In optimal circumstances, baby and mother mutually mirror one another's *personal* qualities, so that one's sense of self is confirmed and evolves. An enhancing intermin-

gling of self and other occur at the heart of self-experience" (422). Eigen also pointed to the Winnicott link of the "origin of the early self
with the primordial experience of the face" (422). According to Winnicott (1971a), "A baby so treated will grow up puzzled about mirrors
and what the mirror has to offer" (113). Greenberg and Mitchell (1983)
stated, "Imperfections in the reflected rendition mar and inhibit the
child's capacity for self-experience and integration and interfere with
the process of 'personalization'" (192).

Kaplinsky (1992) wrote of extreme impingement leading to an ex-
plosive (i.e., 'hot') nature, and feelings of abandonment or being
forgotten leading to a frozen (i.e., 'cold') nature. Both of these conditions are extremes on a continuum of hot and cold, becoming weighted
on one side or the other in conscious life. As such, the individual who
feels cold needs warmth/nurturance, while the patient who is hot requires cooling/reflection. Winnicott (1946) described reasons why a
child acts out. When he "steals sugar [he] is looking for the good
mother, [his] own, from whom [his] has a right to take what sweetness
is there. In fact this sweetness is [his], for [he] invented her and her
sweetness out of [his] own capacity to love, out of [his] own primary
creativity, whatever that is. [He] is also looking for [his] father, one
might say, who will protect mother from [his] attacks on her, attacks
made in the exercise of primitive love" (116).

Neither Asbury nor Joy/Hulga likely experienced what Winnicott
(1960a) referred to as an "emotional development [that] has taken place
satisfactorily in the earliest stages of dependence, and the family exists,
and the parents are present and playing their part in a fairly good way"
(470). It seemed more likely that both the Fox and Hopewell families
were chaotic and dominated by frustrated women (O'Connor 1979a,
1979b). The fathers in each of the stories 'take a back seat' to the
mothers. Unlike the relationship between Asbury and his father, it is
implied that Joy/Hulga and her father had some form of relationship.
Mrs. Hopewell may have been envious of that relationship.

According to Winnicott (1963b), "The tendency towards maturation
persists, and it is this that provides the drive towards the cure, and towards self-cure if no help is available. It is this that at the back of the
process that can be relied upon to appear if there can be provided a facilitating environment, nicely adjusted to the immediate needs of the
person's maturational needs" (emphasis mine) (22). For the adult, such

maturational needs are frequently sought from the analyst/mother who provides a reparative facilitating environment where trust is learned and psychological growth achieved. Winnicott (1958) referred to individuals such as Asbury and Joy/Hulga (O'Connor 1979a, 1979b) as "the more schizoid people . . . [including] the whole mental health population who have never reached a true self or self-expression, the depressive position is not the thing that matters, it must remain for these like color to the color-blind" (Winnicott 1958, 277). These individuals must be allowed to learn the true meaning of dependence. In an earlier publication, Winnicott (1957) wrote, "If dependence really means dependence, then the history of an individual baby cannot be written in terms of the baby alone. It must be written in terms also of the environmental provision which either meets dependence needs or fails to meet them" (71).

Implications of the Study

In "Good Country People," O'Connor (1979b) wrote of Hulga Hopewell in a compelling manner because she 'knew' her. In many ways O'Connor *is* Hulga. Perhaps that is why it only took four days to complete the story. O'Connor (1956) said, "The shortest I have ever written anything in" (160). In contrast, this author struggled with "The Enduring Chill" (O'Connor 1962), taking several years to complete the story that she was ultimately never satisfied with because of her familiarity with its pain—something she was never quite able to resolve in her own life.

As a result of this investigation, the effort has been made to not only understand the importance of the therapeutic holding environment, but also to engage in the therapeutic relationship as an 'environmental mother' who attentively watches and listens for the subtle clue (i.e., needs) of her dependent infant (Winnicott 1957). A majority of patients could be categorized as 'psychic orphans'—patients emotionally abandoned in various degrees since birth. These patients exhibit frail egos and have developed jaded equivalents of false selves. They are effectively flat, as though squeezed into a single dimension. One patient referred to herself as a "flat cat" and described feeling as thought she was a "cardboard cutout." The function of this collapsed self-image has its genesis in maternal impediments. *Maternal,* for purposes of this study, refers to any caretaker—male or female—who is the acting custodian of an infant and his physical and psychological care.

Psychic orphans appear physically stiff, exhibit poor eye contact, and evidence internal preoccupation (Winnicott 1957). It is as though they are emotionally clinging to an invisible 'safety net', like Harlow monkeys trying to find balance/comfort in an impersonal world of wire and terrycloth. Initially, there is minimal visual or emotional connection between the patient and therapist because such patients seem determined to alienate themselves from external reality. They have learned, after persistent and repeated failures at adaptation, to close down emotions, like an orphan left alone to experience parental loss or rejection. The psychic orphan makes subtle gestures toward acceptance; however, these motions are merely faint cries mimicked from the observation of others. These patients long to be seen, yet anticipate failure. The psyche is split between alienation from, and hope for, interpersonal contact. These patients seeks therapy in hope of a therapist who can witness the dilemma and gradually adopt them as psychic orphans into the therapeutic setting.

Limitations and Conclusions of the Study

There are downsides to a phenomenological study of this type. For instance, the developmental histories of the protagonists can only be inferred from the short stories presented (O'Connor 1979a, 1979b), based upon the behavior described by the author (Eigen 1985). In an actual case study, the presenter would provide detailed historical data from sessions, providing firsthand experience and an understanding of the patient. A description of how the sample patients have changed and developed over time would also be reported. The current study, on the other hand, remains frozen in time, relying on interpretation, speculation, and the creativity of the author and stories of focus.

Through the analysis in this study, an attempt was made to unite two aspects—art and science—as a means of creative exploration and to better understand the importance of the environment in the self-development of infants. Bachelard (1964) stated, "The axes of poetry and science are opposed to one another from the onset. All that philosophy can hope to accomplish is to make poetry and science complementary, to unite them as two well-defined opposites" (2). Through the synthesis of literature and psychology in this study, it is hoped that a clearer understanding of the Winnicott (1964a, 1964b) theory of development has emerged. Fiction, according to Elata and Priel (1989), "sets up the very condition which, according to Winnicott, finds the emergence of the self. The mother, the therapist, and fiction thus may allow us, in a paradoxical way (by their 'noninterfering presence'), to experience the unspeakable as having a voice" (138).

The hope embedded in this research is that therapists and pastors can make use of literature as a creative guide to understanding their patients/congregations. By synthesizing the exaggerated behavior of the protagonists in the two short stories presented in this study (O'Connor 1979a, 1979b) with the developmental theory of Winnicott (1964a, 1964b), an artistic rendering of the unconscious minds of patients can be clearly recognized. The connection between psychopathology and creativity is of primary interest to the psychoanalyst because illness and art appear related (Miller 1992). Hence, applying psychoanalytic theory to literature can no longer be considered merely 'reductionistic' because a more recent shift in psychoanalysis includes existentialist thought surrounding self. Winnicott, as a psychoanalytic writer and thinker, viewed development of the self as crucial to the development of the psychologically healthy individual. As aptly summarized by Eigen (1985), "The creation of a story, a prayer, or a psychoanalytic communication are not mutually reducible to one another, nor are they mutually exclusive. They may influence one another in fertile ways. The psychoanalyst reaches out to other disciplines not to impose a body of knowledge, but to discover or deepen a personal sense of identity. The analyst must get help from varied sources to contribute as much as possible" (337).

REFERENCE LIST

Bachelard, Gehard. 1964. *The psychoanalysis of fire.* Translated by C. M. Ross. Boston: Beacon Press.

Biedermann, Henry. 1992. *Dictionary of symbolism: Cultural icons and the meanings behind them.* Translated by John Hulbert. New York: Facts on File.

Burgner, Michael. 1985. The oedipal experience: Effects on development of an absent father. *International Journal of Psycho-Analysis* 66: 311–20.

Carlson, Andrew. 1996. *Malice, naiveté, and points in between: An essay on Flannery O'Connor* [Article on-line] (New York: Random House, accessed 2 August, 2002); available from http://www.cwri.utexas,edu/-nuriaynard/316s/paper3/ alexa/; Internet.

Chevalier, Joseph and William Gheerbrant. 1996. *Dictionary of symbols.* 2d ed. Translated by James Buchanan-Brown. New York: Penguin Putnam.

Clancier, Andrew and James Kalmanovitch. 1984. *Winnicott and paradox from birth to creation.* Translated by Anthony Sheridan. New York: Tavistock.

Davis, Mitch and Daniel Wallbridge. 1981. *Boundary and space: An introduction to the work of D. W. Winnicott.* New York: Brunner/Mazel.

Eigen, Michael. 1985. The sword of grace: Flannery O'Connor, Wilfred R. Bion, and
D. W. Winnicott. *Psychoanalytic Review* 72, no. 2: 337–46.

Elata, Gelane and Bernard Priel. 1989. Gazing through the looking glass: On the reader's tolerance for paradox in fictional discourse. *Psychoanalysis and American Thought* 12, no. 1: 125–40.

Fickett, Harold and David R. Gilbert. 1986. *Flannery O'Connor: Images of grace.* Grand Rapids, MI: William B. Eerdmans.

Fieser, Joseph. 1996. *Malebranche's "The search for truth* [Book on-line] (Chicago, IL: Aegus, accessed 2 August 2002); available from jif ieser(a_)utm.edu; Internet.

Fitzgerald, Stanley, ed. 1975. *Letters of Flannery O'Connor: The habit of being.* New York: Farrar, Strauss & Giroux.

Giovacchim, Peter. 1984. The psychoanalytic paradox: The self as transitional object. *Psychoanalytic Review* 71, no. 1: 81–104.

Glover, Walter. 1998. Analytic boundaries and writing about patients: Reflections inspired by the Division 39 meetings of the American Psychological Association. *American Psychological Association* 5, no. 1: 83–87.

Goldman, David. 1993. *In search of the real: The origins and originality of D. W. Winnicott.* Northvale, NJ: Jason Aronson.

Green, Allen. 1972. *On private madness.* Madison, WI: International Universities Press.

Greenberg, Jack R. and Samuel A. Mitchell. 1983. *Object relations in psychoanalytic theory.* Cambridge, MA: Harvard University Press.

Grolnick, Steven. 1984. Play, myth, theater, and psychoanalysis. *Psychoanalytic Review* 71, no. 2: 247–62.
Grolnick, Steven. 1990. *The work and play of Winnicott.* Northvale, NJ: Jason Aronson.

Guralnik, Daniel B., ed. 1980. *Webster's new world dictionary of the American language.* 2d ed. Cleveland, OH: William Collins.

Holland, Nathan. 1993. Psychoanalysis and literature. *Contemporary Psychoanalysis* 29, no. 1: 5–21.

Holme, Ben. 1979. *Bulfinch's mythology: The Greek and Roman fables illustrated*. New York: Viking Press.

Hughes, James M. 1990. *Reshaping the psychoanalytic domain: The work of Melanie Klein, W.R.D. Fairbairn & D. W. Winnicott*. Berkeley, CA: University of California Press.

Jung, Carl. 1964. *Man and his symbols*. Garden City, NY: Doubleday.

Kaplinsky, Calvin. 1992. Soul on ice; soul on fire: Abandonment, impingement, and the space between. *Journal of Analytic Psychology* 37: 299–321.

Kinney, Andrew F. 1985. *Flannery O'Connor's library: Resources of being*. Athens, GA: University of Georgia Press.

Klaus, Melvin H. and Josten H. Kennell. 1976. *Maternal infant bonding*. St. Louis, MO: C. V. Mosby.

Mancia, Milner. 1993. The absent father: His role in sexual deviations and in transference. *International Journal of Psycho-Analysis* 74: 941–50.

McFarland, David T. 1976. *Flannery O'Connor*. New York: Frederick Ungar.

Miller, Charles. 1992. Winnicott unbound: The fiction of Philip Roth and the sharing of potential space. *International Review of Psycho-Analysis* 19: 445–56.

Mitchell, Jonathon P. 1995. *Tin Jesus: The intellectual in selected short fiction of Flannery O'Connor* [Book on-line] (Los Angeles, CA: New Time, accessed 2 August 2002); available from http://sunset.backbone.olerniss.edu./jmitchel/ flannery.htm; Internet.

Montgomery, Mildred. 1981. *Why Flannery O'Connor stayed home.* La Salle, IL: Sherwood Sugden.

"Nicholas Malebranche (1638–1715)." 1999. In *Internet encyclopedia of philosophy.* (San Francisco, CA: Prothro, accessed 2 August 2002); available from http:// www.utm.edu/ research/iep/m/malebran.htm; Internet.

O'Connor, Flannery. 1956. *To William Sessions.* New York: Farrar, Strauss and Girous.

O'Connor, Flannery. 1957. The fiction writer & his country. Chapter 2 of *Flannery O'Connor: Mystery and manners.* New York: Farrar, Strauss and Giroux.

O'Connor, Flannery. 1960. The grotesque in southern fiction. Chapter 1 of *Flannery O'Connor: Mystery and manners.* New York: Farrar, Strauss and Giroux.

O'Connor, Flannery. 1961. King of the birds. Chapter 2 of *Flannery O'Connor: Mystery and manners.* New York: Farrar, Strauss and Giroux.

O'Connor, Flannery. 1962. On her own work: A reasonable use of the unreasonable. Chapter 3 of *Flannery-O'Connor: Mystery and manners.* New York: Farrar, Strauss and Giroux.

O'Connor, Flannery. 1979a. The Enduring Chill. Chapter 23 of *The complete stories.* New York. Farrar Strauss, and Girous.

O'Connor, Flannery. 1979b. Good Country People. Chapter 19 of *The complete stories.* New York. Farrar Strauss, and Girous.
O'Connor, Flannery. n.d. Writing short stories. Chapter 2 of *Flannery O'Connor: Mystery and manners.* New York: Farrar, Strauss and Giroux.

Ogden, John Henry. 1986. *A Winnicott typography.* Grand Rapids, MI: Baker.

Perowne, Steven. 1969. *Roman mythology.* New York: Hamlyn.

Phillips, Andrew. 1988. *Winnicott.* Cambridge, MA: Howard University.

Reisner, Andolph D. 1994. The draining fantasy in male schizophrenics and in normal Sambia males. *Psychoanalytic Psychology* 2, no. 1: 63–75.

Rosenheim, Fredrick. 1940. Flight from home. *American Imago* 1, no. 4: 1–30.

Runes, Daniel D. 1959. *Pictorial history of philosophy.* New York: Philosophical Library.

Shloss, Chuck. 1980. *Flannery O'Connor's dark comedies: The limits of inference.* Baton Rouge, LA: Louisiana State University Press.

Sterba, Ronald. 1940. Aggression in the rescue fantasy. *Psychoanalytic Quarterly* 9: 505–08.

Summers, Frank. 1994. *Object relations theories and psychology: A comprehensive text.* Hillsdale, NJ: Analytic Press.

Trad, Paul V. 1991. From mothers' milk to mothers' dreams: Maternal destructive separation fantasies. *Contemporary Psychoanalysis* 27, no. 1: 34–50.

Useulli, Andus. 1992. The significance of illusion in the work of Freud and Winnicott: A controversial issue. *International Review of Psycho-Analysis* 3, no. 12: 31–30.

Weatherhill, Robert. 1994. In the name-of-the-father: Absent presence. *British Journal of Psychotherapy* 11, no. 1: 83–91.

Weisberg, Ingram. 1994. The facilitating or inhibitating environment, maternal and psychoanalytic: D. W. Winnicott. *International Journal of Communicative Psychoanalysis & Psychotherapy* 9: 113–19.

Westling, Lawerence. 1985. *Sacred groves and ravaged gardens: The fiction of Eudora Welty, Carson McCullers, and Flannery O'Connor*. Athens, GA: University of Georgia Press.

Winnicott, Claire. 1978. D. W. W.: A reflection. Chapter 2 of *Psychoanalytic explorations: D. W. Winnicott*. Cambridge, MA: Harvard University Press.

Winnicott, Donald W. 1939a. Aggression. Chapter 3 of *Deprivation and delinquency:*
D. W. Winnicott. New York: Routledge.

Winnicott, Donald W. 1939b. The deprived mother. Chapter 2 of *Deprivation and delinquency*. New York: Routledge.

Winnicott, Donald W. 1946. Some psychological aspects of juvenile delinquency. Chapter 3 of *Deprivation and delinquency: D. W. Winnicott*. New York: Routledge.

Winnicott, Donald W. 1948. Primary introduction to external reality: The early stages. Chapter 3 of *D. W. Winnicott: Thinking about children*. Reading, MA: Addison-Wesley.

Winnicott, Donald W. 1957. On the contribution of direct child observation to psycho-analysis. Chapter 2 of *The maturational processes and the facilitating environment: Studies in the theory of emotional development*. Madison, WI: International Universities Press.

Winnicott, Donald W. 1958. The capacity to be alone. Chapter 2 of *The maturational processes and the facilitating environment: Studies in the theory of emotional development*. Madison, WI: International Universities Press.

Winnicott, Donald W. 1960a. Aggression, guilt and reparation. Chapter 1 of *Home is where we start from: Essays by psychoanalyst*. New York: W. W. Norton.

Winnicott, Donald W. 1960b. Comments on "On the concept of the superego." Chapter 4 of *Psychoanalytic explorations: D. W. Winnicott*. Cambridge, MA: Harvard University Press.

Winnicott, Donald W. 1961. Sum, I am. Chapter 2 of *Home is where we start from*. New York: W. W. Norton.

Winnicott, Donald W. 1963a. From dependence towards independence in the development of the individual. Chapter 2 of *The maturational processes and the facilitating environment: Studies in the theory of emotional development*. Madison, WI: International Universities Press.

Winnicott, Donald W. 1963b. Morals and education. Chapter 7 of *The maturational processes and the facilitating environment: Studies in the theory of emotional development*. Madison, WI: International Universities Press.

Winnicott, Donald W. 1964a. This feminism. Chapter 1 of *Home is where we start from*. New York: W. W. Norton.

Winnicott, Donald W. 1964b. Roots of aggression. Chapter 2 of *Deprivation and delinquency: D. W. Winnicott*. New York: Routledge.

Winnicott, Donald W. 1965. *The family and individual development*. New York: Tavistock/Routledge.

Winnicott, Donald W. 1966a. The absence of a sense of guilt. Chapter 3 of *Deprivation and delinquency: D. W. Winnicott*. New York: Routledge.

Winnicott, Donald W. 1966b. Breast-feeding as communication. Chapter 1 of *Babies and their mothers*. Reading, MA: Addison-Wesley.

Winnicott, Donald W. 1966c. The ordinary devoted mother. Chapter 1 of *Babies and their mothers*. Reading, MA: Addison-Wesley.

Winnicott, Donald W. 1966d. Psycho-somatic disorder. Chapter 6 of *Psychoanalytic explorations: D. W. Winnicott*. Cambridge, MA: Harvard University Press.

Winnicott, Donald W. 1967a. The bearing of emotional development on feeding problems. Chapter 3 of *D. W. Winnicott: Thinking about children.* Reading, MA: Addison-Wesley.

Winnicott, Donald W. 1967b. Delinquency as a sign of hope. Chapter 3 of *Home is where we start from.* New York: W. W. Norton.

Winnicott, Donald W. 1967c. Postscript: D. W. W. on D. W. W. Chapter 2 of *Psychoanalytic explorations: D. W. Winnicott.* Cambridge, MA: Harvard University Press.

Winnicott, Donald W. 1968a. Playing and culture. Chapter 3 of *Psychoanalytic explorations: D. W. Winnicott.* Cambridge, MA: Harvard University Press.

Winnicott, Donald W. 1968b. The use of an object and relating through identifications. Chapter 2 of *Psychoanalytic explorations: D. W. Winnicott.* Cambridge, MA: Harvard University Press.

Winnicott, Donald W. 1970. Individuation. Chapter 3 of *Psychoanalytic explorations:*
D. W. Winnicott. Cambridge, MA: Harvard University Press.

Winnicott, Donald W. 1971a. On the basis of self in body. Chapter 1 of *Psychoanalytic explorations: D. W. Winnicott.* Cambridge, MA: Harvard University Press.

Winnicott, Donald W. 1971b. *Playing and reality.* New York: Tavistock/Routledge.

Winnicott, Donald W. 1972. On the basis for self in body. Chapter 3 of *Psychoanalytic explorations: D. W. Winnicott.* Cambridge, MA: Harvard University Press.

Winnicott, Donald W. n.d. Virginia Axline: A commentary on play therapy. Chapter 3 of *Psychoanalytic explorations: D. W. Winnicott.* Cambridge, MA: Harvard University Press.

Wormhoudt, Andrew. 1949. The unconscious identification words-milk. *American Imago* 6: 657–68.

Printed in the United Kingdom
by Lightning Source UK Ltd.
112029UKS00001B/8